Space for Women

A History of Women with the Right Stuff

Pamela Freni

SEVEN LOCKS PRESS

Santa Ana, California
Minneapolis, Minnesota
Washington, D.C.
Helena, Montana

Seven Locks Press
P.O. Box 25689
Santa Ana, CA 92799
(800) 354-5348

Individual Sales. This book is available through most bookstores or can be ordered directly from Seven Locks Press at the address above.

Quantity Sales. Special discounts are available on quantity purchases by corporations, associations, and others. For details, contact the "Special Sales Department" at the publisher's address above.

Printed in the United States of America

Library of Congress Cataloging-in-Publication Data
is available from the publisher
ISBN 1-931643-12-1

Cover and Interior Design by Sparrow Advertising & Design

Table of Contents

Author's Note

The successful introduction of humans into space is one of the brightest achievements of mankind; I feel lucky to have lived during the time this story was unfolding. One day, quite by accident, I discovered that the complete story of the early days of the space program had not been fully revealed in the history books. My desire to contribute to a more complete telling of the race for space by the United States was the genesis of this book.

The Mercury Seven astronauts were arguably the most famous men in the United States and maybe in the entire world during the late 1950s and early 1960s. They were seven of the bravest men this nation had to offer because they were willing to risk their lives to ride a rocket ship into the unknown. They were the elite, the chosen; there were, however, other brave Americans who were for all intents and purposes qualified, and who wanted to become Mercury astronauts more than anything in the world. Despite their credentials and willingness, they were disqualified based on criteria by which none of the Mercury Seven men were judged—they were the thirteen women who had passed the same tests as the Mercury Seven, but were never allowed to see the inside of a space capsule, much less ride one, simply because they were women.

This book is about these women and the events that became part of the collective consciousness of this nation forty years ago, but subsequently were categorized as a footnote and forgotten. As I researched the details behind these women's tribulations, I felt that history had not done its job in chronicling and honoring this unusual story, because then, as now, there is practically nothing recorded and what little public recognition was evident at the time was provided mostly in the "women's section" of the newspapers or in "women's" magazines.

All of the research carried out for this book represents the possibility that there was actually a Women in Space program in two ways. One document presents all phases of testing as being done under the auspices of an authority of the U.S. government; another says it was performed totally privately as a means to pursue a research question. An additional document states, "Both the historical records of NASA and the recollections of those involved in testing women confirmed that the actual role of the women who took the tests was not as candidates for astronaut duty but, rather, as subjects of a study to determine whether women were physically and psychologically fit to travel in space."

On the other hand, the very same document contradicts itself later when it states, "Until astronaut Alan Shepard made the first American flight in May 1961, NASA steadfastly disclaimed any connection with Women in Space training. It was only after his flight, on June 13, 1961, that [Jerrie] Cobb was appointed to her job as consultant to NASA Administrator James Webb." The implication of this statement was that the women's program was real and that this appointment was considered by many people as a tacit admission that the women were in fact being taken seriously as astronaut candidates. They should have been, based on the fact that each test the thirteen took was as hard or even harder than the Mercury Seven's testing regimen.

Considering the secrecy to which each woman was sworn during the testing, I was surprised to discover that there had actually been two days of public Congressional hearings discussing the women's exclusion from the space program. As I searched the local Washington press for records of this event, I had difficulty finding anything until, remembering that it occurred in the early sixties, I flipped to the women's section of the *Washington Post* newspaper. Sure enough, buried among articles on cooking and gardening, I found coverage of the women testifying in Congress about wanting to become astronauts. Because of the lack of acclaim these women's aspirations and sacrifice have garnered, I have sought to record their story for wider dissemination.

Each of these thirteen American women, for two years, were tantalized with a common thought to become the first woman into space. If their foray into the man's world of space exploration had been successful, it might have had an immense impact on the evolution of the space program as well as the nation. In their defeat, however, these women may have done more good by forcing the aviation and space community to begin to grapple with the concept of competent and talented women in the professional workplace. As the thirteen women like to put it, they broke open the doors of space for young women in generations to come. They were as qualified and as fit, or more so, than some of the Mercury Seven; they should have been allowed to go. They had the social and bureaucratic deck stacked against them from the beginning, but they pushed back every step of the way, creating the basis for today's unquestioned inclusion of women into the U.S. space program.

Jerrie Cobb and Janie Hart testifying before Congressional committee in 1962 on the qualifications criteria of U.S. astronauts. (courtesy Library of Congress)

Chapter One

On June 18, 1983, a mere eight minutes and twenty seconds after liftoff, Sally Ride became the first U.S. woman to fly into space when she blasted off on board the Challenger on space shuttle flight STS-7. It was a simple feat; it took only 500 seconds to accomplish, but it had taken the collective voices of millions of women and men and untold years to achieve. Ride, who became a hero immediately on her entry into space, realized that she hadn't come all that way without considerable help from others. "I think I owe a lot to the women's movement. I think I came along, from the point of view of my career, at an excellent time because the women's movement had already paved the way."

Jerrie and Janie looked at each other, totally devoid of energy. The emotions brought on by the despair each of them was feeling were brimming in the women, but they decided not to give in to them. They refused to leave the Congressional hearing room with tears in their eyes, even though they knew that their two-year battle was over. It had been a long and hard two years; now they realized how hard it was going to be to give up their magnificent vision of becoming astronauts. They had both dreamed of the glory that going up into God's country would have brought, where no women and few men had ever ventured. But on July 18, 1962, they had to admit their dream was gone for now. They had had such high hopes just the previous morning that what had once been unthinkable would come to be, based on the confluence of three threads of history that had knitted themselves into a golden river of chance. The imperatives of the women's movement, the Cold War, and the advance of space-capable technology had collided to create a vortex of need so compelling as to have made Jerrie and Janie and eleven other women believe that in 1960 they could serve their country by becoming astronauts alongside men. Some of those very same men had just destroyed their hopes with a few well-spoken sentences.

The day before, July 17, despite the historic significance of the moment, there was no crush of press and very few camera flashes when Janie Hart and Jerrie Cobb went to Capitol Hill. Oh sure, several reporters sat at the usual press table in the hearing room, but no one met them at the building's entrance and very few were even staked out at the door to the hearing room. This didn't surprise Jerrie and Janie much; they knew they were testifying on a subject that was vital to the nation in a way, and vital to them as individuals, but apparently the nation did not want to hear about it. This hearing was the culmination of two years of hard work and political maneuvering and they were both very nervous. They knew that if they lost this battle the entire war was over for them and eleven other very talented women. Who wouldn't be nervous? They were testifying in front of a subcommittee of the U.S. government on the groundbreaking, win-all or lose-all battle they were waging to bring women into the U.S. astronaut corps.

As they waited for the proceedings to commence, Janie noticed that this was one of the small hearing rooms. It was disappointing to realize that the subject at hand did not even rate one of the large hearing rooms most often seen on television newsreels. As she waited, she also wondered what qualifications beyond her experience anyone could possibly want from her before allowing her to serve as an astronaut.

Born in 1921, by the time she testified Janie Hart had been a licensed pilot for nineteen years and had over 2,000 hours of flying time, most recently in her twin-engine six-passenger Aero

Commander airplane. In addition to fixed-wing flying, she was the first woman to be licensed as a helicopter pilot in the state of Michigan and was, she proudly noted, the twenty-fifth woman in the free world to have attained that license. She had been a captain in the Civil Air Patrol back in Michigan, all the while participating in numerous national competitive cross-country air races. The races had such names as the "Powder Puff Derby" but there was no fluff to competing in one of them. It took endurance, planning, and brains even to finish one of those races.

In June 1943, she married the man who was to become a noted U.S. Senator from the state of Michigan. As her husband Phillip Hart completed his military service and embarked on his political career, he and Janie became the parents of eight children, four girls and four boys. She helped him get elected as lieutenant governor of Michigan—twice—by assessing the areas where she could provide the most assistance and diving in with enthusiasm. When Phil decided to run for the U.S. Senate, she once again evaluated his most pressing need and learned to fly helicopters so she could pilot him in short hops all around the state, thereby overcoming a name-recognition problem with the Michigan electorate. She added this to a whirlwind of activities she maintained in her home state, including piloting Rose Kennedy around when Rose arrived on the campaign trail for her son John's presidential bid. When Phil won his Senate seat for the first time in 1959, she packed the family's possessions and moved the entire household and eight children to Washington, D.C. At this point, traveling into space would have, no doubt, seemed easier.

At the age of forty, she was the oldest of the thirteen women who had successfully completed a major portion of the screening testing used by NASA for qualifying astronauts. She knew she had been recommended for inclusion into the group for many reasons, including her amazing physical condition after having given birth to eight children. All of the women involved knew that arguments that women who had undergone the rigors of childbirth were not physically fit for space travel would inevitably arise, and she was living proof this was not true.

Janie was dressed for business in a blouse and skirt; her hair was short and stylish. As she waited for the hearings to begin, she surveyed the members of the subcommittee. Even though she had not met them all, she knew who each of them was: Victor L. Anfuso of New York (chairman), Joseph E. Karth of Minnesota, J. Edward Roush of Indiana, William F. Ryan of New York, James C. Corman of California, Joe D. Waggonner, Jr., of Louisiana, Corinne B. Riley of South Carolina, James G. Fulton of Pennsylvania, R. Walter Riehlman of New York, Jessica M. Weis of New York, and Alphonzo Bell of California. She spotted no known friends of their cause, but no known enemies either. She was afraid the enemies would surface in the list of people scheduled to testify later in the hearings. She knew, in addition to herself and Jerrie, that the experts scheduled to be called included Jacqueline Cochran, preeminent female pilot in the United States; Scott Carpenter and John Glenn, U.S. astronauts; and George M. Low, Director of Spacecraft and Flight Missions, Office of Manned Space Flight at NASA. These hearings had been officially established to hear testimony on the qualification criteria for astronauts, but ultimately, Janie thought, were going to prove to be a debate on why women were not able or, better yet, not allowed to qualify as astronauts. She wondered at the fact that less than sixty years ago the Wright brothers had just mastered the art of flying; here they were now, sitting in a room talking about sending a woman into space. She knew that not long after Orville and Wilbur had launched themselves from a windy dune in North Carolina, women had followed. In 1910, just eleven years before Janie was born, Blanche Scott became the first American woman to solo in a fixed-wing aircraft. In 1911, Harriet Quimby became the first American woman to earn her pilot's license. It amazed Janie that in such a short time, so many things had changed for the country and for women. She was glad because she knew that she wanted to be the next Scott or Quimby in space travel.

As she thought about it, she realized that space was the obvious next stepping-stone for the nation; she was here to make sure women were allowed the same access to space as men. During World War II, the combat requirements of two major theaters of war demanded that so many men leave this country to defend it that for the first time in U.S. history women were called to work en masse to ensure that factories, businesses, and services continued to function at full capacity. Previous wars had required women to step up into the unusual territory of daily work. During the Civil War and World War I, a number of women had worked in support of the troops, but they had done so in a much smaller proportion. But now, women had no choice but to go to work in huge numbers in order to keep their fighting men fully supplied with food, equipment, and weapons. The work was new and interesting to them and created many exciting avenues for women as independent wage earners. Hundreds of thousands of women joined the workforce in response to the labor shortage. Before the war, women in general were not considered breadwinners, but their country needed them now. Unemployment was almost nonexistent as every able-bodied American went to work. Through their willingness to give up their home life and go to work, women became the daily guardians of the fighting men as well as of the country's economy. They drove trucks, they built bombs, they rolled up their sleeves and did everything that had to be done, everything that men had done before them.

Out of this effort came the image of Rosie the Riveter, considered by some as the first commercial depiction of mass careerism by women in this country. Even though hiring women was an economic imperative for industry to survive the loss of all the men to the war, the change was met with a sense of surrealism, as though everything happening was a dream or at the very worst only a temporary condition. The nation considered wartime as calling for unusual efforts, but that things would return to normal at the conclusion of the war—it was not glorious, it was just what one had to do—and it changed the women.

In a commentary of the time, Mike Royko of the *Chicago Tribune* saw the change and commented on the difference in women's outlooks. "Suddenly I saw something I hadn't seen before. My sister became Rosie the Riveter. She put a bandanna on her head every day and went down to this organ company that had been converted to war work. It became more than work. There was a sense of mission about it." The mission for many women had to do with the realization they could become, professionally, complete, contributing individuals. It wasn't what they had in mind from the start, but simply evolved as an outcome of working outside the home in jobs they liked and for which they were well paid. The World War II era is considered a watershed moment in our country's history as far as workforce demographics are concerned. It was a point when women began to think of themselves as career owners. The media began to urge the country's young women to think of their contributions to the industrial workforce when they came of age. Working became such an accepted practice for all women that by the war's end, there were hundreds of thousands of them in the workforce. Salaries for women in some geographic areas had doubled between 1939 and 1944.

This was the first time significant numbers of American women were given a taste of workforce equality, and they liked it. They wanted to have careers and earn their own money, but more than that; these women, who were just stepping out of a centuries-old role the culture had told them they were predestined to fulfill, also wanted to have the same kind of freedom men experienced. They were left with the totally novel and refreshing concept that they could function competently in the noisy, dirty, hardware-oriented world of men.

Once they tasted independence, they wanted fervently to contribute to all professions, engineers, architects, generals, and even pilots.

In addition to the shortage of commercial manufacturing and service workers, another problem that surfaced during the war was a shortage of home-front military personnel who could run the day-to-day business of war. In response to this critical shortage, in 1942 (after a fierce debate in Congress) women were allowed to become military auxiliaries. The nation's leaders had not wanted women exposed to the rough ways of life in the military workplace, but common sense and a dire need prevailed. Women worked as office personnel, typists, and any other positions that freed an able-bodied man to get on with the more dangerous calling of war. The press was curious about these women, but had no basis for stereotyping them as professionals, so they wrote about what they knew best: clothing and makeup.

This type of reporting was to become an endless and tiresome trend as women stormed each new bastion. The women's talents were almost totally disregarded by the press in favor of subjects to which the reading public could relate. Much newspaper ink was devoted to their new uniforms: the fit, the undergarments, and the skirt length. These military uniforms were characterized as "lumpy" and speculation abounded as to whether a girdle was necessary government equipment for these uniformed women. Many were banned from businesses because some of them wore pants rather than skirts. At one point, a pants-wearing group was barred from boarding a train because the conductor was totally unconvinced of their morality. Many of them, while in uniform, were mistaken for airline stewardesses.

In addition to ground-based military jobs, some women flew in service of their country. The lack of men on the home front resulted in an acute shortage of pilots to accomplish local military flying duties. After Pearl Harbor, the military could not keep up with the demand for combat pilots, much less the number of pilots required to do the daily chores for the country of delivering supplies, ferrying planes

from factories to air bases, and flying targets for gunnery practice. The
need for additional pilots to meet this emergency was made public
and patriotism compelled 25,000 women to volunteer to be military
pilots. Requirements included a high school diploma and 500 hours
of flight time. For the exact same duty, men were required to have
three years of high school and 200 hours of flight time.

Despite the obvious insult, women volunteered anyway, and they
flew every type of aircraft in the American war arsenal from 1942 to
1944, from B-29s to the smallest and fastest fighter aircraft. Some performed test flights for newly engineered planes while others did less
glamorous, but no less important, aircraft delivery flights. Despite
their talents and timely contributions and even though the war effort
desperately needed them, the country couldn't quite get used to the
idea of women military pilots.

An article in *Look* magazine dated January 9, 1943, summed it up
in a single sentence: "The United States has found it hard to believe
that women make good pilots." But it was a golden era for women
aviators. Thousands of them had taken to the skies and they proved
to be very good pilots. As the war ground on, many of them held jobs
teaching flying to men who then replaced pilots at the war fronts. The
concept of earning a living as a pilot was capturing the imagination of
many young women throughout the United States, driving them to
become just like the women they heard about and saw in the newsreels.

One young woman, Myrtle Cagle, was being encouraged by her
mother to become an independent thinker. As she would recall many
years later, Myrtle looked up to her mother as a role model; she noted,
"She was the first woman in our town to drive a car." Myrtle took her
mother's admonitions to be independent very seriously and was constantly on the lookout for different, unbeaten paths to follow. A few
years later, Myrtle was destined to become involved in an effort that
was at the pinnacle of women's independence.

There were innumerable barriers to overcome, but many women managed. A set of twins who lived in California, Jan and Marion Dietrich, were taking what had up until then been a male-only class for ground school—the preliminary step toward earning a pilot's license. Another girl from Oklahoma, Geraldine Cobb, was (at the age of twelve) learning to fly an airplane with blocks tied to its foot controls so she could reach them. Hundreds of others were making their way to dusty airfields all over the country and beginning what would turn out to be a lifelong love of flying. It was a privilege for which many fought because women pilots were so unusual.

With the war ending, by 1946 the men had returned from the battlefront and thousands of women's jobs were lost as the wartime military establishment was dismantled and men began to reassert their cultural dominance over the workplace. The women of this era were also products of their culture which stated that despite the fact that many women had just spent four years working outside the home, women as a whole should not have career expectations. An agonizing debate tormented the country in the months after the war ended, discussing the pros and cons of whether women should be allowed to continue in their jobs or if the returning soldiers deserved those jobs more; some women could "do the job" just as well or better than men. The ultimate conclusion of this debate was that men deserved jobs more than women. Most women were sent home or back to low-level jobs, ones that did not pay as well as those they were abandoning. As the legions headed back home, however, all the women internalized the experience of being competent and kept something important firmly gripped in their minds—it never went away; "Rosie" had a newly found freedom and she wasn't going home to stay forever. The familiar patterns of the prewar years had been broken. This awakening was one of the most important episodes in the historic epic of women's rights, second only to winning the right to vote in 1920.

Jerrie and Janie had been raised in circumstances that made them
believe there were no differences between men and women while in
the pilot's seat. Jerrie's father loved to fly and was instrumental in her
breaking free of the earth and learning that only in the sky was there
true freedom. He served in the army and dreamed of qualifying for
the Army Air Corps. The family lived in Witchita Falls, Texas, when
he bought a Waco biplane with an open cockpit to hone his piloting
skills. Up until then, Jerrie had eyes only for horses, but after the first
time in the air, nothing else in her life was important except flying.
She waited anxiously for her father's return from work each day so
they could go up into the great blue sky. "I'd make sure the plane was
all gassed and oiled and waxed, so when he got there we wouldn't
waste time on the ground."

During the period that women were "manning" the front lines of
the nation, the war ground on with many surprising consequences.
Something new was on the horizon, and it was both exciting and
frightening. Prior to World War II, the Germans had been working on
the development of a rocket-boosted space vehicle. Now it seemed
they had made a breakthrough of monumental proportions.

Rockets had been around in some form since approximately 1045 A.D.
They evolved from cylinders tamped with gunpowder in China into
somewhat more sophisticated weapons used during the ensuing years
throughout the world. Introduced into Europe around 1300 A.D., rocketry made it to the New World by the early 1800s during the War of
1812. There were many attempts at using this new technology, and
one quite large rocket was even used during the American Civil War
to try to bomb Washington, D.C., from Richmond, Virginia. Until the
1940s, the performance of all rockets was effectively hampered by the
type of fuel used as propellant. This was about to change.

In the twentieth century, two of the greatest minds in the history
of rocketry grappled with this problem and began research programs
half a world apart, each unknown to the other. Robert H. Goddard,

an American, began studying rockets and solid fuel use in 1919, while a German, Wernher von Braun, started to do so in the 1930s. By December 1934, von Braun was in the employ of the German army and with the vast resources afforded by that sponsor, he was successful in creating a liquid propelled rocket; ethanol and liquid oxygen were used as fuel. The rocket was designated the A2. Research and development continued and he created another, improved version called the A3.

World War II intruded; instead of the rockets being used as research projects as originally intended, the German army and von Braun began to toy with them as a solution for delivering long-distance destruction to the Allied forces of the West.

On October 3, 1942, after two previous failures, von Braun led the German scientists at Peenemunde, Germany, on the island of Usedom in the Baltic Sea to successfully launch the first missile to penetrate outer space. They didn't realize it at the time, but the Germans had developed the embryo of what was to become the instrument of a space race that would take place years into the future. This rocket, the A4, was renamed the V-2, and known as the Vengeance-2. This was the rocket bomb used to destroy much of London and kill many of the English population during the final years of World War II. While its completion came too late to affect the outcome of the war, over 3,000 V-2 bombs were launched to damage London and other Allied cities. Thousands of people were terrorized and killed and tens of thousands of buildings were destroyed because of this weapon.

When it became apparent that the war was going to end badly for Germany, von Braun and his team of more than a hundred scientists were reportedly marked for assassination by their own Nazi government so that this enormous brain trust would not fall into the hands of the Allied victors. In late January 1945, a secret meeting was held between von Braun and his most trusted associates. As if the assassination rumors were not bad enough, the scientists determined that their location lay directly in the path of the approaching Russian army. They thought of nothing except continuing their research into rocketry, and in discussing the latest threat, decided that a life spent serving their Russian captors would not be in their best interests.

A unanimous vote among the group determined that they should remove themselves into an area of the country where capture would more likely be by the Americans. They were inadvertently helped along their way when the German military ordered them to retreat from their current position near the coast of Germany to a more central location where work on the rockets could continue. Despite his efforts, it became almost impossible to keep the entire team together and occupied with meaningful research, but von Braun and his greatly diminished team persevered. The assassination rumors became stronger, forcing von Braun and his brother to try harder to find a way out of danger. It became apparent to all that the closer to the Americans they could maneuver themselves, the better off they would be.

They hid their most important technical documents to ensure that they would have a trump card and control who would receive this technical treasure trove at war's end. As the walls of war continued to close in on them, their German handlers moved them deeper into the mountains, away from the fighting.

Finally, the Americans came close enough. On May 2, 1945, the younger brother of Wernher, Magnus von Braun, was chosen by virtue of his limited understanding of English to go into the countryside and contact the advancing Americans. He found them, and after some linguistic somersaults arranged for the Americans to take custody of the German "rocket men" just inside of Austria. First Lieutenant Charles Stewart was initially skeptical of what he was being told, but acted on Magnus's entreaties out of curiosity. Because he did, he alone was probably responsible for snaring the greatest collection of intellectual property the entire war had to offer, all for the benefit of the United States.

As the war wound down, hostilities ended and an era of overt war was concluded. A new era of mistrust and suspicion, called the Cold War, commenced. Daily propaganda was more powerful than the bombs and bullets of the just-concluded war, and a time of great danger began between two newly emerging superpowers, the United States and the United Soviet Socialist Republic (U.S.S.R.).

During the final days of the war, both the United States and the U.S.S.R. benefited from the concept of "to the victor go the spoils." The Germans had made exceptional progress in their research and development of rocket vehicles, and after the capture by U.S. forces of tons of equipment and most of the German personnel, all the people and hardware were relocated to the United States through a secretive and convoluted travel itinerary. The German team was first sent to Ft. Bliss in El Paso, Texas, then finally to White Sands Proving Grounds in New Mexico, where its members continued refining their ideas side by side with American scientists through the early 1950s. The original V-2 technology created in Peenemunde provided the basis for the vehicle that would put an American into space and proved to be the prototype of the one the United States would use to put a man on the moon. A supercharged V-2 rocket was the launch vehicle for not only Alan Shepard, but also Gus Grissom, two of the Mercury Seven astronauts who broke the space barrier for the United States.

The United States was not alone in its efforts to send manned, rocket-propelled vehicles into outer space. The U.S.S.R. had also captured significant amounts of research data and hardware explaining the German secrets.

In fact, the aftermath of World War II, with the numerous technological advances it brought in both rocketry and weaponry, resulted in an international certainty that space would be the next battleground between the superpowers; the nation that owned this piece of high ground would have an enormous strategic advantage over everyone else. This new battleground was an important feature of the Cold War that began to form between the United States and the U.S.S.R., with both superpowers flexing their technological muscles, showing each other and the world who was superior.

The space race between the United States and the U.S.S.R. became a significant arena in which international opinion of dominance was formed. Each country was aware that it was participating in an opera of sorts on the international stage of world politics. Space exploits were becoming the next tally sheet by which to recount whether we were "keeping up with the Joneses," or in this case the Russian version, the Joneskis. Daily newspaper articles excitedly discussed the latest breakthrough made by each country. American children were taught how to respond during missile attacks by the U.S.S.R. Dinner-table conversation often centered on the fears of what might happen if the "Reds" attacked America.

The United States was falling far behind in using the technology the Germans had masterminded because without any warning, on October 4, 1957, the 184-pound *Sputnik I* was blasted into space by the U.S.S.R. It was the first satellite to have ever orbited earth. The American public was stunned and suddenly frightened. Despite all the work being accomplished at home with the Germans' information, the Russians had made the first breakthrough. The politicians were furious. In this day and age, when many of our services are routinely provided to us via satellite, it's almost impossible to convey the complete trauma, and for some, the terror of having a Russian satellite orbiting overhead.

Up to this point in the nation's entire history, not a single enemy vessel had ever approached the United States that was not successfully challenged and repelled. Subsequent to the launching of *Sputnik I*, this was no longer true. American soil could now be spied on or attacked at will and nothing could be done to stop it. Making matters even worse, there was certain knowledge by now that the Russians had also learned the secret of creating nuclear weapons; the combination of the two technologies would be deadly if they ever chose to use it.

Real fear was instilled in the general population throughout the nation for the first time and for years to come, because these two facts made it evident that the U.S.S.R. had the technology to inflict serious damage on our homes and loved ones with impunity. Space exploration advocate and Senate Majority Leader Lyndon Johnson echoed the sentiments of the population in a written account of the effects of this event: "In the open West you learn to live closely with the sky. It is part of your life. But now, somehow, in some new way, the sky seemed almost alien."

Personal recollections of the author's parents worriedly viewing the night sky evening after evening during that crisp October, trying to catch a glimpse of this new object, are still vivid memories. It seemed to them that Johnson had been correct; the New Mexico sky was now somehow different.

By nature a deliberate man, President Eisenhower did not let the one-time event of *Sputnik I* divert him from his planned path of leading the country toward measured successes in space travel and exploration. His advisers agreed to this studied approach and suggested he laud the Soviets for their achievement, but not to make too much of the importance of a single satellite in space. Several days after the *Sputnik* launch, Eisenhower held a press conference to discuss the event. He mentioned that a single satellite of very limited capabilities was no threat to the United States. When asked why he had let the U.S.S.R. beat us in the race, he replied that he didn't consider it a race and that no one had ever suggested to him that it should be: "[I]n view of the real scientific character of our development, there didn't seem to be a reason for just trying to grow hysterical about it."

This was not what the American public wanted to hear. It wanted a president who was willing to go toe to toe with the Russians and be first into space. There was a huge backlash from the populace in the face of the president's comments. Eisenhower's lack of willingness to be stampeded by what he felt was basically a circus trick by the Russians turned out to be one of the major miscalculations of his presidency. He failed to "appreciate the psychological dimension of launching the first satellite. Far from being about science solely, *Sputnik* came to be about the way Americans saw themselves."

To Eisenhower's credit, he had been carefully moving the country's infrastructure toward a comprehensive space program. Planning teams had long been in place that were wrestling with the issue of whether the military or a civilian organization should control the space program. Teams were concerned with planning a studied program intent on providing scientific outcomes and not political products. All these problems and many more were being tackled by an organization called the National Advisory Committee on Aeronautics (NACA). NACA was responsible for the execution of research in aviation in the United States and was led by General James Doolittle.

Doolittle became famous during World War II and known as a free-thinking risk taker. He seemed the perfect leader for this endeavor. The general had been flying almost since the advent of airplanes and in 1922 made history by being the first person to fly across the country in less than twenty-four hours. Additional fame had come his way as the pilot who led the first successful raid on Tokyo in World War II.

As the U.S. program was being planned, and much to the dismay of the nation, on November 3, 1957, *Sputnik II*, with Laika the dog on board, was successfully launched and orbited by the U.S.S.R. The world was in awe—this was proof that the first launch had not been a fluke and the Russians truly had the knowledge to successfully repeat the process at will. Not only had they launched another satellite, the Russians had been able to send a live animal into space before the United Stateshad even launched a rocket with a payload equivalent to *Sputnik I*. The only comment with which America could counter this public affairs coup was a show of horror that they had launched Laika into space with absolutely no intention whatsoever of bringing her home: "Godless Communists! Besides being the enemy, they were also dog killers."

The second launch was a major Cold War victory against the West. Finally stampeded, President Eisenhower moved to counter the two successful Russian launches with a successful American launch. In a major address on November 7, 1957, he used the nose cone of an Army Jupiter-C missile as a prop, proving to the nation that U.S. scientists had overcome reentry problems for ballistic bodies. Soon, he ordered U.S. forces to prepare to launch an American satellite by December 6, 1957. His usual orderly approach to the presidency and the space program had been overwhelmed by public relations concerns. His natural tendency was to maintain the nation on a steady course of completion of space projects for the good of the country, not for some splash in the local paper, but the groundswell of reaction from the population in general was such that it seemed prudent to provide some answering thunder from the United States.

The rocket was readied, but to the shock and disappointment of the nation it exploded just as it cleared the launch pad in early December. The press nicknamed it the "Kaputnik," or alternatively the "Stayputnik" in total disgust. The payload had been a 33/4-pound test satellite that the Russian leader Khrushchev derisively called the "orange." During the rest of December 1957 and most of January 1958, Congress, the public, and the technical aviation community agonized over the country's lack of a rocket engine large enough to push anything sizable into space without exploding.

With the U.S. technology available, the payloads had to be diminutive in order to leave the earth's gravitational pull, but finally on January 31, 1958, the America's first satellite, the *Explorer I*, with a payload of 18.13 pounds, successfully orbited the earth and discovered the presence of a radiation belt around the earth (today known as the Van Allen Belt). Weeks later, the *Explorer II* failed to reach orbit.

On March 17, 1958, another small satellite orbited. The *Vanguard I* was on a survey mission and proved to the world that the earth was shaped more like a pear than an orange. Even though it sent back important data, this payload was a tiny fraction of the size of the 1,120-pound *Sputnik II* payload.

On May 15, 1958, *Sputnik III*, a satellite weighing nearly 3,000 pounds, was orbited by the U.S.S.R. At the time, this payload was considered enormous. The United States still had no rocket engines large enough to hurl a payload even remotely similar into space. On August 17, 1958, an attempt to launch another U.S. rocket carrying an unmanned probe to the moon was made. Carrying a payload of 40 pounds, it exploded a few miles downrange in a spray of fire and despair. The ghost of Russia continued to haunt the engineers and scientists charged with getting the United States. into the space race. Ten days after this disaster, the Russians launched an even larger vehicle containing two dogs that they successfully recovered upon the spacecraft's landing.

As the race continued and the public relations consequence of each success or disaster was played out in the world press, a new player, a national space organization, was being organized in the United States. Previously, the American rocket and space program, with a few exceptions such as NACA and the president's Science Advisory Committee, had been run as a purely military effort. Now an organization was created to centralize all research and development efforts occurring within the government into a single civilian organization.

In 1958, in response to Public Law 85-568, President Eisenhower established the National Aeronautics and Space Administration (NASA) and made it responsible for all civilian space activities in the United States. Over 8,000 people, five major facilities, and $340 million were transferred from various NACA venues to the agency. This new organization was civilian, but part of its job was to be a counterweight to the Russian military's space launch successes. The hopes of the nation were that this centralization of effort would produce "more bang for the buck" while imparting a sense of professionalism and direction to the world of peacetime space exploration, as well as to ultimately create a space program capable of answering the Russian expertise. It was supposed to focus the entire team of American scientists on a single mission—to find a way to pull even with the Russians in the space race.

Other American attempts to launch rockets with various payloads were unsuccessful in October, November, and December 1958; even with NASA taking the reins, the Russians kept showing us up. On January 2, 1959, in another first for the U.S.S.R., the Russians successfully launched a rocket, *Lunik I*, carrying nearly 800 pounds of scientific equipment, into solar orbit. The seemingly unending string of successful launches and large payload sizes by the Russians amounted to a figurative tongue wag at the United States. We were taking a public relations beating in the space race and had no way to counteract it. Finally, in March 1959, the United States launched a lunar probe, *Pioneer IV*, with the final destination of solar orbit. Even though it was viewed with pride by the United States, it contained a pitifully small payload of 13.4 pounds and had the dubious distinction of once again being the *second* craft to leave the earth's gravitational pull on a solar mission behind the Russian's first.

While there was public pressure building on NASA to create a credible technical program, there was volcanic-level pressure building up in more private scientific circles between the manned flight program and the scientific community. Throughout the time the United States played catch-up with the Russians, an abyss was growing between proponents of manned flight and those who thought electronic and scientific payloads were better. Manned flight was to most Cold War fighters the obvious step to counteract the Russian propaganda. Sending a human into space was a way to bring the public into the process and play to its romantic concept of the questing spirit of man. To members of the scientific community, however, sending a man into space was a waste of time and payload space. They argued that scientific instruments could do a far better job of analyzing the findings of space and would not have to be retrieved.

The frailty of the human spirit was also often cited by scientific purists as the weak link in the concept of manned space travel. They maintained that instruments had no emotions or weaknesses to consider. On the other hand, the proponents of manned space exploration argued that without a human aboard to intervene, malfunctions and unexpected consequences would doom mission after mission. As more and more studies were undertaken to prove this argument and determine the type of person that could maintain control during space flight, it became obvious that women were equally if not better suited for the isolation and hardships of space than men.

Studies proved women were far superior to men at maintaining alertness and facing the reality of prolonged isolation and were emotionally more fit for the rigors of space. Women were also favored because they live longer and weigh less. The longevity of women's lives also proved to be a plus supporting a future vision of very extended manned voyages to the outer planets of our solar system. In the 1950s, it was believed that these journeys would become commonplace within the foreseeable future. The weight factor was a potential solution to the contemporary launch problem of pitifully small payload capacities. It cost about $1,000 per pound to launch a payload into space at this point in the space program. (Today that figure is closer to $10,000 per pound.) Fifty pounds per launch (the difference between a man and a woman) could make a significant cost difference. If a human was to be boosted into space as a payload, the payload had to be as small as possible to reduce the cost and guarantee success.

As this debate continued within the scientific community, NASA forged ahead with launches, focusing on small victories. On May 28, 1959, fully a year and a half after the first Russian launch and recovery of an animal into space, the United States launched two monkeys named Able and Baker more than 300 miles through the atmosphere into space. But on October 4, 1959, the second anniversary of *Sputnik*, a Russian spacecraft was launched which would later photograph the far side of the moon. On March 11, 1960, the United States launched a satellite bound for Venus. The space race became like a tennis match, back and forth, with lobs and counterlobs. On August 19, 1960, the Russians successfully launched an earth-orbit spaceship holding numerous animals. This proved to be another extremely irritating first for the Russians; it was called the flying zoo and elicited comments from an envious U.S. scientist: "Next thing you know, they'll have a soccer team and a Mack truck up there."

As the Russian space successes continued to pile up, the U.S. administration commanded the space experts to do something to balance the international tally sheet between the two superpowers. As the book *This New Ocean*, written by Loyd S. Swenson, Jr., James M. Grimwood, and Charles C. Alexander, notes, Russian accomplishment in space was driving the U.S. to weigh in on some plane in the space race. "[P]ublicity and public interest had reinforced each other until the manned program clearly had become the most promising hope of 'beating' the Russians into space."

Chapter Two

Plans were finalized and put underway to select the first U.S. astronauts who would represent a human presence in outer space. Initially, the records of 508 military personnel were screened; 110 (five from the Marines, forty-seven from the Navy, and fifty-eight from the Air Force) of these men were judged adequate for continued consideration. Through attrition (many of those contacted declined, choosing to stay with their military careers) and testing, that number was pared down to thirty-two. These thirty-two men were then sent to the Lovelace Foundation for Medical Education and Research, Department of Aerospace Medicine, in Albuquerque, New Mexico, for exacting physical examinations. Only one was disqualified through these exams from continuing to the next set of tests.

The remaining thirty-one candidates were then sent to other venues throughout the United States for psychological and physiological endurance testing. One of the most harrowing exams that all of them underwent was the sensory deprivation test. This consisted of depriving the subject of all sensory inputs for hours on end by enclosing him in a totally dark and silent room. It took its toll on many of the candidates, according to Dr. Don Kilgore of the Lovelace Clinic, who said recently that many of the men were unable to bear this isolation and were eliminated during the conduct of this test.

According to the official accounts, the finalists (the Mercury Seven), were chosen solely based on the results of these physical tests as well

The Mercury Seven astronauts—(left to right, front row) Wally Schirra, Jr., Donald "Deke" Slayton, John Glenn, Jr., Scott Carpenter, (left to right, back row) Alan Shepard, Jr., Virgil "Gus" Grissom, and Gordon Cooper. (courtesy NASA)

as additional psychological and stress tolerance aptitude tests. Lesser known was that when the attrition rate was too low to select a team of the requisite number of astronauts, all the test results were thrown by the wayside and, according to evaluation committee leader Charles J. Donlan, the committee resorted to "looking for real men." He noted that the selection tests had actually been "tests of tests," creating a body of research data to try to formulate what future astronauts might be like; no test was a definitive qualifier or disqualifier. This concept was to become very important a few years later when women were tested for qualification as astronauts. After extensive and rigorous examinations, seven men were proffered as the best that the country had to offer.

In an announcement on April 9, 1959, NASA noted that seven men had been chosen to train for the Mercury space missions, including the first U.S. manned space flight. The "Mercury Seven" were John H. Glenn, Jr., Virgil I. "Gus" Grissom, Alan B. Shepard, Jr., Scott Carpenter, Gordon Cooper, Walter Schirra, Jr., and Donald "Deke" Slayton. These men were to represent the United States and the intense hope of the nation was that an American would be the first human to ever go into space.

Of the seven, Alan Shepard was chosen to be the first to fly an American ship into space; the populace waited tensely to see if the United States could beat the Russians in accomplishing this one, huge step. Tension surrounding the "first man in space" milestone was plainly visible in the aeronautical industry as well as throughout the nation. All involved were working long hours and pushing themselves to their physical limits. Tom Wolfe wrote in *The Right Stuff,* "NASA engineers and technicians at the Cape were pushing themselves so hard in the final weeks people had to be ordered home to rest."

The rocket scheduled to carry Alan Shepard into space was on the launch pad and everyone was almost ready when it was announced that on April 12, 1961, Yuri Gagarin had orbited the earth in *Vostok I.* General Donald Flickinger, member of the National Aeronautics and Space Council and Assistant Deputy Commander for Air Research and Development Command, was at Cape Canaveral briefing a visiting group from the United States Air Force Office of the Surgeon General about the prospects of an American first when he was handed a note informing him that the United States had lost yet another race.

According to the account of a witness in the room at the time, Flickinger, who didn't have to elaborate, said simply, "They've got a man in orbit." Gagarin was the first human in space, and he was a Russian. One of the greatest international public relations plums had just been picked by the Russians, and the United States was left without an answering ploy.

According to *This New Ocean* authors Swenson, Grimwood, and Alexander, the very next morning both NASA administrator Jim Webb and deputy administrator Hugh Dryden were present at a command performance on Capitol Hill and were "roasted before the verbal fire of the House space committee as they were asked to explain what had happened." Despite the fiery atmosphere in the hearing room, they basically told Congressmen James Fulton and Victor Anfuso that the United States had lost this part of the space race long before NASA had come into existence. This wasn't much of an answer, but it was apparently correct. Not at all satisfied, Representative Joseph Karth summed up the feeling in Congress by saying, with an air of implied criticism, that the two countries had taken two different routes to the same destination. "The Soviets had pretty much rifled their program as opposed to the United States shotgunning their effort." President John Kennedy was far more philosophical: "We are behind, the news will be worse before it is better, and it will be some time before we catch up."

NASA was supposed to be bearing the fruit of success based on the fact that the agency had requisitioned the best talent that the military, scientific, and engineering communities had to offer while developing, as the *Astronaut Selection and Training for Manned Space Flight* manual stated, "the largest systematic and sustained peacetime research and development effort ever undertaken by the United States." This effort was second only to national defense in the amount of budget it consumed and the importance it took on in the national consciousness. Despite all of this, for years to come if you had written the following headline with a fill-in-the-blank—"Russians Put the First _____ into Space"—you could have just about summed up the space race from

October 4, 1957, until December 24, 1978, when the United States finally did something first by putting humans into moon orbit. As one article described the pain the country was feeling, "It happened to be the late 1950s at a time when American school kids were learning to count '3-2-1-dammit!' as our rockets blew up on the pad, while the Soviets routinely boosted theirs into orbit."

The first orbiting satellite, living creature, and man in space as well as an unmanned orbit of the moon were Russian victories. During the Cold War, propaganda firsts were critical to the prestige of the winning country. To some these accomplishments, and the possible technological advances they represented, also served as deterrents against aggression between superpowers. The Russians were gathering all of these bragging rights.

As pressure on the space community mounted, promises of a space race coup were made to President Kennedy and the country by NASA. These promises were finally kept when on May 5, 1961, Alan Shepard became the first U.S. citizen to be blasted into space. His flight reached 115 miles into space and traveled 302 miles total, on a flight that lasted fifteen minutes. It took place three weeks after the Russian flight, but it might as well have been a lifetime.

Despite of, or maybe because of the successful Shepard flight, the administration took matters into its own hands and President John Kennedy stunned the nation, and more important, NASA, by promising that there would be an American man on the moon before the end of the decade. On May 25, 1961, after months of searching for a space achievement that would produce dramatic results, Kennedy told Congress the nation should and would take the helm in the space race and show the world that we were a nation of achievement rather than failure. He said, "Now is the time for this nation to take a clearly leading role in space achievement, which in many ways may hold the key to our future on Earth." This promise was made before we could predictably launch a rocket without having to destroy it when it went berserk after launch, and it was long before we could even begin to envision putting a man on the moon; the scientists and engineers at NASA had been given an impossible task.

Behind the scenes, the people in charge knew that the trauma of frequent and repeated failure was creating a national public relations crisis, and that the United States needed something or someone to help us out. As each headline reporting an American failure or Russian success added pressure on NASA, the United States was becoming desperate to gain a first in the space race. During the frenzied response to all the unexpected Russian success, the proponents of the U.S. space program grasped for anything that would lead to a public relations equalization of the space race. This desperation drove some people to do something that would at least even the public relations score with the Russians, if not better it. The U.S. space program had to succeed in something that was so superior and so outrageous the world would forget the technological shortcomings and the failures of the previous few years. After the Gagarin flight, one of the few notable feats left in the public relations grab bag was putting a woman into space before the Russians could send up a chorus line of females. This idea sparked a suggestion in some quarters to allow women into the testing process for the astronaut corps, women who had only managed to gain Rosie the Riveter status less than twenty years before.

Chapter Three

Janie Hart was surprised to find herself and Jerrie in this room testifying before Congress. Even though angry when their astronaut tests
had been cancelled, she had not, despite rumors, used her unique
position as the wife of a U.S. Senator to petition members of Congress
for a public hearing. On reflection, she thought her husband, Senator
Hart, had engineered the hearing, but she had never put him on the
spot by asking.

She was glad to have Jerrie Cobb at her side. An enormously talented pilot, Jerrie would make a good technical impression on the
members of Congress as well as the press. Janie knew Jerrie had been
through all the training and testing available and yet still was not an
astronaut, making her a perfect example for discussions about why
women were being excluded from the astronaut corps.

Jerrie was outwardly self-assured and beautiful as she waited for
the beginning of the hearings, her golden hair swept into a ponytail
the way she always wore it. Her dark-blue dress and heels matched,
and her large white necklace and earrings showed off her femininity
perfectly. The heels must have worn thin during the day, because one
news photo shows her feet hiding under the table—with shoes flung
aside. Jerrie was probably wondering how a girl from the Oklahoma
countryside had made it all the way here, testifying before Congress.
Always more comfortable in the air than anywhere else, this was the
last place on earth she had been prepared to go. Despite her air of

calm and quiet at the table, before the hearings began she confessed to Congressman Anfuso that she was scared to death about testifying. Going into space would have been supremely easy compared to speaking in front of Congress.

She and Janie knew they were fighting outrageous odds to become astronauts, but even after two years, they relentlessly continued the battle because there was still a smidgen of a chance of winning.

Jerrie had been willing to fight from the first time she had ever heard of what she knew about the Women in Space program.

Chapter Four

In 1959, the space programs of both the United States and Russia considered sending a woman into space. A totally new subject for contemplation, this provided a point of contention in the U.S. space program: which country could or would send the first woman into space? Thousands of questions immediately presented themselves for answers, questions such as, "Is it ethical to send women into space? Can their fragile emotional and physical states withstand a trip into space?"

Shortly after completing the medical screening of the Mercury Seven astronauts in 1959, Doctor Randolph Lovelace II of the Lovelace Foundation in Albuquerque, New Mexico, heard through the international grapevine that Russia had admitted women into its astronaut program and was in the process of revving up the propaganda machine one more time for another first by preparing a woman for space. His competitive spirit and natural curiosity compelled Dr. Lovelace to want to do more than merely consider the question of women's suitability for space—he wanted answers.

He was a natural for this effort. He headed the original human factors and training subcommittee for NASA that in 1957 considered and established the scientific and biomedical requirements for manned space flight. With his guidance, this NASA subcommittee had functioned as the key group of people who planned and implemented the first astronaut selection program. In an earlier effort, he had been involved with establishing high-stress biomedical requirements when he and his staff from Lovelace Clinic supported the physiological, high-altitude testing done on all the pilots who flew the U-2 spy airplane. This experience gave Dr. Lovelace enormous insight into what the space medicine community thought constituted the makings of a good astronaut, man or woman. His idea of putting a group of women through the exact same set of tests the Mercury Seven had undergone would ensure that there would be an evenhanded understanding of the fitness of women for the rigors of space.

The Mercury space flight tests were accomplished by the Air Force School of Aviation Medicine, an umbrella organization that used several government medical facilities such as the Lovelace Clinic. The first phase of testing required of the Mercury candidates was exacting and included in-depth baselining of all physiological structures, for a total of seventy-five different tests. Blood tests determined the oxygen-carrying capacity of each person's blood, and centrifuge examinations analyzed the blood's serums. There were urine tests, stool tests, gastric tests, and cholesterol analyses. Liver function tests, urinary steroid excretion analysis, blood nitrogen, blood protein, protein-bound iodine, and special serum studies were done. All sorts of X-rays were used to ensure each person was as perfect as a human body could be. A pint of radioactive water had to be swallowed in conjunction with the X-ray testing. Eyes were tested for every known affliction. Ears, noses, and throats were tested, as were hearts. One of the tests consisted of swallowing a three-foot portion of a rubber hoselike device. Nerves and muscles were also tested, including riding a bicycle to the point of collapse.

Hundreds of questions were proffered to determine whether the candidates had ever had supernatural experiences or whether they had ever experienced paranoid delusions.

Everything imaginable had to be tested, because no one really knew what the human body's reaction would be at the point where one entered "space." Almost every scientist in the United States had an opinion; most thought it was going to be very difficult, maybe even deadly.

On earth the atmosphere is 20 percent oxygen and 80 percent nitrogen. As an astronaut approaches outer space there is increasingly less oxygen until at 40,000 feet, for all intents and purposes, there is none. Pressure on the surface of his body is so slight that long before an astronaut arrives in space, specially designed suits are needed to supply oxygen and pressure to keep the body's fluids from boiling. Theories current at the time generally designated the seventy-five mile point as where "space" began; no one knew how the human body would react past this point. The available data was so new that debate surrounded even this simple point—when is one actually "in space"? In a 1958 White House memo discussing the exploitation of outer space, the definition of "outer space" caused considerable consternation: "As a matter of fact, no acceptable definition has yet been evolved as to where 'air-space' and 'outer-space' begin and end." To draw a parallel the memo used conditions familiar to earthbound people, that of maritime law. It noted that maritime considerations have "no such problem [determining if you are at sea or not] because, under most conditions, one is either afloat or ashore. The limits of the 'high seas' have been determined by international agreement on the basis of very easily made physical measurements. With respect to outer space, however, such questions are wide open."

Additional concern centered on the cardiovascular system's capacity to function adequately in weightlessness. Earthbound hearts use gravitational pressure to help pump blood. The system's compensation to a zero-gravity atmosphere includes reduced output of effort. The result of what space-induced cardiovascular laziness would mean to an astronaut was unknown. All these variables and potential reactions had to be tested during the astronaut screenings so the astronaut's life was not endangered by a single undetected physical flaw.

To answer the questions plaguing him, Dr. Lovelace began searching for a single woman with the right credentials who would agree to undergo the grueling testing process. He found her in Geraldine

"Jerrie" Cobb. Born in 1931, she had a genetic imperative to fly. Her father was a pilot who taught her to soar at a very early age in an era in which women pilots were not the norm. Jerrie was a flyer's flyer; she had great instincts and, moreover, a great love for the act of being free when she flew. She loved the breaking of earthly bonds and the feel of the wind beating at her face. She flew for the first time at the age of twelve in a biplane rigged with blocks on the pedals in order for her to reach the controls. She received her private pilot's license at such a young age that, by contrast, today's teenagers would only be worrying about a driver's license.

Geraldine earned her commercial license in 1949, when she was eighteen years old. Shortly afterward, she applied for a flying job in Florida using her nickname, "Jerrie." The company hired her from afar and she used her last bit of money to drive to her new job. On arrival, her gender was discovered and she was told that women could not be pilots for hire. Having no money, she was forced to take a job available just down the hall as a clerk. A few months later, however, she proved her detractors wrong and continued her career by becoming an international ferry pilot as well as a test pilot.

Over the next several years she gained experience in piloting at least sixty-four different types of airplanes, including a jet fighter and a four-engine turboprop. At the time she was asked to join the Women in Space program in 1959, she held a distance record; during the next few years she would achieve speed and altitude records for several different types of airplanes. When Dr. Lovelace met her, she was assistant to the vice-president for Aero Commander, Inc., an executive-aircraft manufacturing company in Oklahoma. Her commercial license included multiengine, flight instructor, and DC-3 captain ratings, and she was also qualified as a ground instructor in navigation, meteorology, civil air regulations, aircraft, and engines. Remarkably, she had logged over 10,000 hours of flying time.

An all-American girl, she seemed to be the perfect astronaut candidate. Dr. Lovelace immediately recognized in her the qualities for which he was searching when they met by chance in September 1959. Jerrie was on a marketing trip for Aero Commander in Miami when she was introduced to two men, both of whom she recognized as having significant positions in the Mercury space program—Dr. Lovelace and General Donald Flickinger. Just returned from a conference in Moscow, the two men were certain the Russians were moving toward launching a woman into space. After learning of her flying credentials, they broached the subject of an American woman going into space. As she heard what they had in mind, Jerrie's heart soared at the thought of training to become an astronaut. Over the next three or four days she and the two men met several times to discuss the possibilities and probabilities of the existence of enough women in the country who might be interested in such an adventure. Based on her own enthusiasm, she reassured the men that there would certainly be enough women available if they could just get a program underway. As she was leaving Miami to return to Oklahoma City, both men agreed they would check her credentials and let her know if they wanted to take the idea any further. On the off chance it might come true, she agreed to present herself at the Lovelace Clinic whenever Dr. Lovelace was ready.

Barely five months later she found herself in Albuquerque, New Mexico. Beginning on February 15, 1960, at the Lovelace Clinic Jerrie went through several days of the most rigorous physiological testing available in the world at the time. She started the week in high spirits, but as the testing ordeal became onerous her spirits began to fail. In an effort to help, a member of the clinic testing physicians, Dr. A. H. Schwichtenberg, prescribed a night out for her as his family's dinner guest. To Jerrie's delight, one of the other guests at dinner was General James Doolittle, along with his wife. The former chairman of NACA, General Doolittle served on the President's Science Advisory

Committee and was well acquainted with all the space race efforts. He had early on become a proponent of manned space flight.

Jerrie had admired General Doolittle from afar, as had most of the nation, so meeting him while she was testing to become an astronaut seemed a very positive omen. Jerrie's book, *Woman into Space*, relates that during the course of the evening's conversation, the general spoke to her of the importance of the effort in which she was involved. He said, "What you're doing is good, Jerrie. Keep it up— make it work." Support and concurrence from such a prominent American with Lovelace's testing for women was just what she needed to lift her spirits. As she wrote later, "When General Doolittle tells you to do something, you exert every conceivable effort to do it."

Jerrie returned to the testing schedule the next morning rejuvenated and more determined than ever to do herself proud. She needn't have worried; her test results showed she passed without any problems and she was most definitely astronaut material. As a matter of fact, she was considered highly motivated and she positively impressed everyone with whom she came into contact. Dr. Don Kilgore, who was the ear, nose, and throat specialist at the clinic conducted many of the tests on Jerrie, later said she passed all the tests "admirably." Each of the examining doctors considered her an outstanding candidate for space travel.

As she endured each test, clinic personnel reassured her that she was being subjected to exactly the same suite of tests by which the Mercury candidates had been judged. (Throughout this book the three suites of tests are discussed as "phases." Phase I consisted mostly of physiological testing and occurred at the Lovelace Clinic. Phase II consisted of psychological testing. Phase III consisted of flight-conditioning testing. This terminology is used only for ease of discussion and was not common phraseology at the time.)

This baseline testing was considered the most complete and grueling physical examination ever given to a woman, and Dr. Lovelace was pleased with what he saw. He believed, like other proponents of the manned space concept, that the core of space exploration was going to be based on humans' in-the-moment capacity to use their intellect. This, he believed, would prove to be much more valuable than strength or manual capability. Mental acuity would lead to intellectual verbal communication and descriptions that would be very critical to the dissemination of the experience and value of space. These beliefs and Jerrie's test results gave him confidence that if they were allowed to go into space, women would be able to do the job as well as anyone.

Jerrie's physical condition and overall attitude were considered excellent and she was recommended to the Aeromedical Laboratory in Oklahoma City for stress tests—phase II of the astronaut training process. During her medical outbriefing at the Lovelace Clinic, Dr. Secrest commented on her remarkable physical conditioning wishing there were more women like her. A few months later, Dr. Secrest was delighted to find there were several more just like Jerrie.

Despite a lack of popular national appeal for the idea of a woman astronaut, later that year Dr. Lovelace reported, "Jerrie demonstrated a point that many scientists have long believed; that women may be better equipped than men for existing in space." Dr. Lovelace continued by explaining that women have lower body mass and need significantly less oxygen and less food; hence, they may be able to go up in lighter capsules, or exist longer than' men on the same supplies. Since women's reproductive organs are located internally, they would be able to tolerate higher radiation levels without serious damage. Jerrie's outstanding results in phase I broke the barrier and recommendations were made that other women be tested to see if they could pass the astronaut physical. Studies throughout subsequent years have repeatedly concluded that men and women differ little in their ability to adapt to the biomedical stresses of space. In fact, studies indicate that women are probably slightly superior to men at weathering the combined stresses of space travel.

In search of qualified women in addition to Jerrie, Dr. Lovelace enlisted the help of his friend and aviation hero Jacqueline Cochran to determine if enough American women pilots were willing to be tested in the same manner as Jerrie. Cochran was asked to become involved in the effort, in part because she had stellar credentials and knew the best women pilots. Also significant was that she and her husband had previously provided generous financial grants to the Lovelace Clinic. Dr. Lovelace evidently wanted to find the best women to test as well as ensure that if there was additional financial need, Cochran (who at this point in her life was a very wealthy woman) would be generous with the clinic, as she had on previous occasions.

A driven individual, Jackie Cochran helped those whom she believed could do something for her in return. The Lovelace Clinic was at the center of the qualification process for space travel; if Jackie had any designs on becoming an astronaut, she would most assuredly need friends at the clinic where important decisions were being made about astronaut selection.

With decades of flying experience, Jackie had already earned more honors than most male pilots in the world; from this viewpoint she would be an excellent judge of the quality of the piloting skills of each woman being considered. Her working knowledge of the capabilities of the most experienced women pilots in the United States came from her command a few years previously of the Women's Air Force Service Pilots (WASPs) of World War II.

During World War II, Cochran served as part of the General Staff of the Army Air Force Training Command in Texas and later as part of the General Staff of the Air Force, with headquarters in Washington, D.C. In that capacity, she helped originate the concept of women pilots in the military and screened, selected, and trained many of the women who made up the WASP units during World War II. She was also the wife of Fred Odlum, who served as the head of the Atlas Rocket Company and was a close friend of and campaign contributor to President Franklin Roosevelt. For her efforts in creating, training, and supporting the WASPs, Jackie was awarded the Distinguished Service Medal. This experience made her an influential and knowledgeable source for determining which women might successfully navigate the astronaut testing. Additionally, as Dr. Lovelace might have guessed, her international reputation and her interest and support of a program gave it immediate credence and, based on her well-known circle of friends in Washington, a cachet of officialdom.

Jerrie provided a list of names, which along with Cochran's list was used to determine the identity of twenty-three of the most outstanding women pilots in America. In a letter from Dr. Lovelace, each one was asked if she would be willing to fly for her country, albeit in an entirely different way than she had ever done before. The women were told this was the beginning of "the Women in Space program" and each of them was requested to endure all the necessary testing in total confidence so the program could be carried out without the glaring lights and expectations brought on by the press's presence. When the pilot wife of the lieutenant governor of Michigan heard through a friend that these invitations had been sent, she called Lovelace and wrangled one for herself; that made twenty-four. The candidates came from all walks of life and even though it was grossly inconvenient for many of them, both personally and professionally, they all volunteered without reservations to begin what Dr. Lovelace called the determination of the qualifications of women as astronauts.

The twenty-four women were asked to report to Albuquerque for testing in late 1960 and early 1961, singly or in pairs. Once again they were asked to ensure that all testing was carried out in total secrecy. Most attended by paying their own way, but in a few cases, Cochran was called on to provide financial assistance when money for a hotel room or airplane ticket ran short. She later reported that she paid

$18,000 from her personal funds to ensure that all twenty-four candidates could participate in the testing process. Though this was a significant sum at the time, she seemed more than willing to support the effort to the fullest, ensuring that the space program and the country got what they needed for success. Her life had been spent trying to convince the men of the world that women could do anything men could do; this seemed a great arena for continuing her quest.

On July 16, 1962, Congressman Anfuso, the chairman of the subcommittee, promptly opened the hearings at 10:00 A.M. with words that must have been very gratifying for Janie and Jerrie to hear. His statement emphasized the consequences of space exploration for the country and that no human resource could be left unconsidered based on "the fact that these talents happen to be possessed by men or women. Rather, we are deeply concerned that all human resources be utilized."

Jerrie's testimony was eloquent, but unwavering. Obviously frustrated, she pointed out that the group of thirteen women had long been seeking a public forum and in an obvious swipe at NASA she declared, "the courtesy of a hearing has not been extended to us by any other branch of the Government." Many of the women had spent weeks of their time and hundreds of their dollars trying to find a way to answer what they were sure was a call from their country, and Jerrie wanted everyone to know about it. Her entire mission in seeking this forum and testifying before it was finding a place in space travel in which women would be allowed to participate so they would have a place in American and world history.

As testimony began, she provided a history of the women and of all the testing they had undergone. Until this time, the women's names, locations, and qualifications had been kept as quiet as possible. "Now you may ask, who are these twelve women, always referred to, but never identified? Why don't they get together and let themselves be heard? The answer is easy. They don't even know each other." Each had complied gladly when told that keeping the testing secret might help all of them get a shot at the program. It had been difficult, but all of them had met the terms of their agreement. "Because the scientists involved and I have spent several years awaiting some word from governmental circles that the women would be included in the official astronaut training program, we asked the girls for more than a year to keep their identities under wraps."

Jerrie continued her testimony about the testing process, noting that half the twenty-four participants had results equally astounding as hers. From very diverse backgrounds, the women came to this program with many dreams and hopes; twelve passed the tests with dreams intact. Adding Jerrie to the list made thirteen who had passed the first phase of the astronaut testing, some turning in results superior to the Mercury Seven.

Geraldine "Jerri" Sloan Truhill was a starry-eyed girl when she saw her first WASP in uniform and her life changed forever. In the third grade she decided to become a pilot and from the moment of that chance encounter with the WASP, she wanted to fly in the service of her country. The only divorcée in the group, she was born in Texas, the child of an Amarillo oilman. Raised in a dusty patch of north Texas, she would have found it easy to dream of flying an airplane away into another, more beautiful land. As the mother of one, she was one of the few women being tested who had children. She and Bernice Steadman went through the Lovelace Clinic exams during the same week. Each night after the completion of the tests, she and Steadman would compare their experiences. Undoubtedly they compared notes on questions asked of them during the day, wondering why it was important for them to answer the question, "Who am I?" A vertigo test during which the physician squirted freezing water into their ears until they became dizzy undoubtedly proved to be another favorite. (Jerri has often said she had no secrets after some of those tests. They were so thorough that she was sure some of the doctors

knew things about her that she didn't even know.) She flew for an aviation company and had a commercial pilot's license with multiengine,
instrument, and flight instructors ratings. She had over 1,200 hours of flying time. Despite knowing that failing these tests would not rob her of
her livelihood, she wanted desperately to become an astronaut and
decided she simply would not bomb out. She was a lifelong proponent
of the right to succeed or fail based on her own merits; being a woman,
in her opinion, shouldn't disqualify one for anything.

She flew an astounding array of large airplanes and was proficient
at the controls of B-25s, B-26s, and DC-3s. She was blessed with an
open and sunny disposition; the kind which persists until faced with
injustice. To this day, she remembers her outrage when she heard a
story, credited to one of the Mercury Seven astronauts, commenting
on the inclusion of women on space flights. This shortsighted man
reportedly said that each astronaut was being allowed to take along
ninety-five pounds of recreation equipment, implying that women
could certainly qualify as "recreation."

Jerri's testing partner, Bernice Steadman (or "B" as she likes to be
called), also felt women were boundless in their abilities. Married and
the owner and operator of an aviation service, she was approached
to participate. Like Jerrie Cobb, she learned to fly before she could
drive, and she also loved to sail. She had an airline transport pilot's
license with multiengine, flight instructor, instrument instructor, and
ground instructor ratings. Despite long days at work, she managed to
amass an impressive 8,000 hours of flying time. She and Janie were
great friends and she was the one who told Janie about the Women
in Space tests so she could join in on the fun.

Gene Nora (pronounced "Gennora") Stumbough Jessen had a college degree, a relatively unusual credential for a woman of this era.
Additionally, she had attained a commercial pilot's license with multiengine and ground instructor's ratings. As a professional pilot, she
flew for a large aircraft company in Kansas and had 1,450 hours of

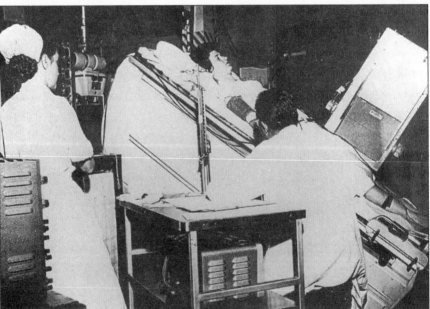

(Top) Gene Nora Jessen in a 1962 promotional photograph while flying for Beech Aircraft factory. (Bottom) Jessen on tilt table at Lovelace Clinic in 1961. (courtesy Gene Nora Jessen)

fixed-wing flying time. She was at the Lovelace Clinic in the spring of 1961 with Janie Hart. They endured the endlessness of the tests together and, according to Janie, "laughed their way through adversity." These tests in adversity included drinking a pint of radioactive water for one test and drinking twelve ounces of barium for another. Janie said that as she was undergoing a pelvic examination during the testing, the doctor was so amazed at her high level of conditioning after eight children, "that he practically called a staff meeting in the examining room" so intent was he in sharing his discovery with his staff. She is still today an amazingly fit individual.

Jan Dietrich went through preflight class at the age of sixteen and began to amass flight time as soon as she got her license. A few years later, she became a flight instructor, authorized by the FAA to issue pilot's licenses. One of the first women in the United States to earn her airline transport pilot rating, her logbook showed an impressive 8,000 hours of flying time. A college graduate, she also held an airline transport pilot's license with multiengine, single-engine seaplane, and flight instructor ratings and had used these credentials to become a pilot for a large company in California.

After she received her letter from Dr. Lovelace requesting that she prepare to report to Albuquerque, she began a physical training regimen, just to be ready for whatever was in store for her. Serious aspirations to qualify obligated her to rent a stationary bicycle and she began to race in place mile after mile to improve her stamina. She and her twin sister, also a candidate, sought the counsel of a doctor who had advised Olympic athletes. He changed their diets to steak and other high-protein foods. Deep knee bends strengthened her muscles and swimming fifty laps at a time enhanced her endurance. After months of waiting, she finally became convinced the letter had been a false alarm and that the final summons was never going to arrive. A month after she abandoned her training regimen, she was called to report to the Lovelace Clinic.

She wrote her twin sister, Marion, each night with news of the day's tests. Also scheduled to be tested soon, Marion perused each of Jan's letters, knowing that Jan's experiences would provide her with significant preparatory information. Marion waited anxiously in California and read each letter with pleasure. They told her of a full week of early morning starts and rushed days. Jan told her, "Come with a little extra weight; you miss one or two meals every day." Finally, Jan wrote the letter Marion had been waiting for: " I have passed the tests."

Marion Dietrich was thrilled with the thought that if she passed, she and Jan might become astronauts together. She had earned a college degree in psychology and a commercial pilot's license with seaplane and flight instructor ratings and she had 1,500 hours of flight time. As with almost all twins, the two were very close. At the age of sixteen, Marion and her sister took the physical exam required to apply for a pilot's license. They qualified for the airline transport pilot's rating, but were told this didn't matter because those particular certificates were never issued to women. After gaining special permission to attend the boys-only high school class, she attended preflight class at the same time as Jan. Now she was going to do what the boys were doing, only this time she didn't need special permission.

Marion, like Jan, remembered the exact date—September 14, 1960—when she had received a letter asking if she'd be interested in participating in initial examinations for women astronaut candidates. She was stunned as she read the first few words of the letter; it asked, "Will you volunteer for the initial examinations for women astronaut candidates?" The letter continued by stating that the testing was voluntary and would take one week. Afterward, she would not be committed in any way to the Women in Space program unless she desired to be. Her hands trembled as she read the signature, Dr. W. Randolph Lovelace II, Director of the Lovelace Foundation. She knew the foundation was the epicenter of "the most important air event in history," and here was a letter asking if she would be interested in participating. Recalling the fourteen-hour days she and Jan had worked in the post office to earn money for flying lessons, she remembered all the lessons they had taken and the joy they felt on earning that first little piece of paper, their pilot's licenses. All the achievements had been hard fought, and now here was another little piece of paper tapping her on the shoulder. She was ecstatic and wanted nothing more than to serve her country.

Two months passed with no other contact. Marion was beginning to worry. Finally, a few weeks after Jan completed her tests, she was told to report in two days to the Lovelace Clinic in Albuquerque. When she checked into the designated hotel, the manager began giving her a pep talk so she wouldn't fret. According to him, his pep talks were the only thing that kept most of the women in the tests from going straight home. "Why, the girls today, they were like to quit, but I talked them into stayin', too." She wasn't afraid of the tests; she just wanted to be sure she passed them. Like all the other women as they approached the testing, fear of the unknown was quickly replaced by the much greater terror of failing.

Jan had been correct when she had warned of the hectic pace. The schedule noted that if time permitted, Marion could have breakfast, but time never seemed in the mood to permit. She worked to ensure that throughout the days of endless testing her outward attitude was always positive and cheerful. Unspoken criteria during the tests included cheerfulness in the face of adversity; capacity to compensate for stress engendered by the tests was graded and became a focus point in the final analysis.

Marion's attitude was severely challenged when the second day's test involved swallowing three feet of what looked like a very long balloon. It was part of the gastric testing, but seemed to be part of a torture chamber. (The existence of this test is surrounded with controversy. Dr. Kilgore, one of the original physicians at the Lovelace Clinic, denies it existed. At least three of the women, in completely different venues and without consultation, recount the test in very similar terms shortly after completing phase I testing.) Marion fell into the same letter-writing habit that Jan had begun, reporting on each day's tests. The letters she wrote and received during the times both twins spent in Albuquerque served as gentle supports, each for the other, through the tests when the times got tough. Finally, it was all over except for the results.

She was relieved and thrilled when told she had been successful. When it was announced that both Marion and her twin had passed all of the tests in phase I, her boyfriends reacted with a myriad of opinions ranging from "it's inappropriate" to marriage proposals. One who had wanted to propose to her was now thinking the better of it. Another was rattled when a newspaper article noted that the colonization of space was imminent. "Is that what they might use you for? Let the scientists dig up their own women." She didn't care about any of the comments; this was a chance to represent her country in a patriotic way. If it cost her a few boyfriends, it was okay. Her father's reaction, though, was totally unexpected. Instead of being against it, he wanted to go in the place of one of the twins. An aviation buff since he had helped build a glider in his childhood, he was saddened that there was an age limit, so fascinated was he with space. Marion, an established writer, and Jan, a professional pilot, returned to their jobs with the hopes that soon one or both of them would be called on to go into space.

Another of their testmates came from a state far away from the twins' sunny California home. Thirty-one-year-old Rhea Allison had been born in Minnesota, but was living in Texas when she was contacted. Her brown hair and blue eyes belied the quiet but strong woman with a college degree and 1,500 hours of flight time. She served as an executive pilot for an aircraft engineering firm and she had her commercial pilot's license with multiengine, single-engine seaplane, flight instructor, instrument instructor, and ground instructor ratings. Previously a schoolteacher, she had decided flying was more in line with her professional aspirations. With her teaching credentials, Rhea's endeavors to become an astronaut during 1960 would have nullified efforts by the United States to send a teacher into space on the ill-fated 1986 space shuttle *Challenger* flight on which teacher-in-space Christa McAuliffe died.

As Jerrie continued recounting the credentials of each of the thirteen women to the subcommittee, she was only able to note a few points about each woman. Mary Wallace "Wally" Funk deserved more than just a few words. Born in New Mexico, she attacked every endeavor with enormous intensity. A nationally ranked snow skier of Olympic caliber, she was also the

(top) Wally Funk at Ft. Sill, Oklahoma, catching a ride in a T-33 at the beginning of the Mercury Thirteen program; (lower left) Wally at age eight; (lower right) Wally flying a Cessna 310. (courtesy Wally Funk)

first woman flight instructor at Ft. Sill, Oklahoma, where she taught flying to Army officers. She had a degree from the University of Oklahoma and a commercial pilot's license with single-engine seaplane and flight instructor ratings. With 3,000 hours of flight time, she worked as a professional pilot, and at the age of twenty-one was the youngest of the thirteen women. As usual, her intensity and competitive style carried over to the astronaut testing. With each endurance test, she often produced results superior to the Mercury Seven.

Jean Hixson, the second oldest of the troop, held the best educational credentials of them all. She had undergraduate and master's degrees in math, physical sciences, and psychology, augmented with a commercial pilot's license with multiengine, instrument, and flight instructor ratings. As a schoolteacher with 4,500 hours of flying time, she also could have been the first teacher in space.

Myrtle "K" Cagle confesses her earliest memories are of wanting to fly. One of four within the group of thirteen who was married, she was in college and was a pilot at an Air Force base. Her sense of humor demands she tell the story of her first flight. As a three-year-old, K watched a sparrow hop on the ground and then take flight. She was intrigued with the little bird's freedom and set about trying to duplicate it. Using her mother's umbrella as a parachute, Myrtle took a flying leap off the roof of her front porch in Selma, North Carolina, and went crashing to the ground. Although she carried a scar on her face for years to come, she never regretted her "maiden" flight.

At the time she was licensed in North Carolina, K was the youngest person in the state to receive a pilot's license. When she flew a jet in 1953, she was one of approximately five women in the United States to have ever done so. She had an airline transport pilot's license with multiengine, flight instructor, instrument instructor, and ground instructor ratings. She had, at one time, operated an airport and had 4,300 hours of flying time.

Irene Leverton boarding a Stearman biplane in 1949. (courtesy Irene Leverton)

Irene Leverton was another Californian, and, as an executive pilot, she held an airline transport pilot's license with multiengine land and seaplane, instrument instructor, and flight instructor ratings. She has said she was born wanting to fly and with over 9,000 hours of flying time, it seems as though she has spent most of her life in the air. Because there was a moratorium in place against all nonmilitary flying on the West Coast during World War II, the Civil Air Patrol, considered quasi-military, was the only practical way for Irene to become an experienced flyer. She soloed in 1944 as a CAP cadet during her third year of high school. When the inquiry came from Dr. Lovelace, Irene was flying twin-engine airplanes for an air taxi company in Southern California. She was sacked for requesting time off to go to Albuquerque. Without a job and short of money, she was one of the beneficiaries of Jackie Cochran's financial support of the program.

Sara Gorelick Ratley was the last on Jerrie's list of astronaut aspirants. She held a college degree in mathematics, physics, and chemistry and a commercial pilot's license with glider, multiengine, single-engine seaplane, flight instructor, and instrument instructor ratings. She had begun, for a woman of this era, an unusual career working as an engineer for AT&T, all the while racking up 1,800 hours of flying time.

Along with Jerrie, these twelve made up the Mercury Thirteen. They proved to be a varied lot in education, residential location, marital status, and age. They finished the tests of phase I successfully and were sent home to wait until it was their turn to take part in the next test phase, sure that with the results they had been able to attain they would be the next citizens allowed to defend America's honor in space.

Chapter Five

Jerrie's success during the physiological testing in Albuquerque garnered her an invitation to phase II testing in Oklahoma City. Although September 1960 was her start date for the next battery of tests, a few weeks earlier she was invited to the Lewis Research Center in Cleveland, Ohio, to be tested in the multi-axis spin test inertia facility (MASTIF). Although this was not a part of the "phased" testing, Jerrie considered it a chance to demonstrate her mastery of an additional test simulating conditions that she might confront in space. It was also an opportunity to add another credential to her dossier in case there was a question of her withstanding the level of acceleration expected when a spacecraft lifted off. It was so unusual for women to be tested in this machinery that it is possible she was the very first.

Jerrie's first glimpse of the MASTIF filled her with awe: "The device is a gigantic, three-way gyroscope. Its tubular metal cages take up about as much space as the average two-story house." It was designed to test an astronaut's ability to control all possible attitude manifestations: pitch, roll, and yaw. The book *This New Ocean* described early reporters' reactions to the machine in an approving voice, noting the "extraordinary contortions of the MASTIF, billing it the ultimate in wild carnival rides."

Jerrie, strapped into a couch about the same size as her body, struggled to control the beast when the MASTIF was released, as it began to buck and roll at the same time. Considering three different attitude corrections simultaneously is difficult for the brain, but after only minutes, she had gotten the machine under control. As told in *This New Ocean,* Alan Shepard's first ride in the MASTIF was a little different from Jerrie's. "When the MASTIF finally started to spin, Shepard turned green and pressed the red 'chicken switch,' sounding a claxon horn as a signal to stop."

Jerrie tamed the MASTIF exceptionally quickly, so the handlers let her have another go at it. After her experiences there, she left thinking she could handle just about any challenge this astronaut adventure could throw at her; she could not know that things were only about to become interesting.

In August 1960, Dr. Lovelace presented a paper at a Stockholm medical meeting discussing the results of Jerrie's tests, as well as disclosing her identity. He said Jerrie had qualified to "live, observe, and do optimal work in the environment of space, and return safely to earth." Subsequently, Jerrie was besieged by the press, all of whom wanted to be the first to interview the person who was widely hailed as the leading U.S. candidate to be the first woman in space.

This presentation not only named Jerrie; it had let the proverbial cat out of the bag about the women's program, and public opinion began fueling the debate on women in space. Speculation was rife in this space-obsessed era as to what the first American woman in space would be like. *Look* magazine published an article that included speculation about the physical attributes of the ideal woman astronaut as "flat chested, lightweight, under thirty-five years of age, and married." The article went on, saying her personality would "soothe and stimulate others on her space team." Everyone was convinced this woman would be unable to go into space on her own merits, but would probably be "the scientist-wife of a pilot-engineer."

At first Jerrie wasn't allowed to talk freely to the press. *Life* magazine had previously sniffed out her involvement in the Lovelace Clinic tests, but in trade for an exclusive interview with her at the right time had agreed not to break the story until given permission. This agreement forced Jerrie to stall all other members of the press until after *Life* got its article. Her stalling just stirred the reporters into a frenzy, and she was stalked by the media so relentlessly that she hid at her parents' home for days to deter some of the hounding. Frustration mounted among the reporters, who were not to be denied, to the point that in order to force the issue, one British publication threatened to create a national uproar by saying Jerrie had been kidnapped by the Russians.

A few days later, at a press conference arranged by *Life*, she felt as though she was about to be the press's main course. She was afraid the press would revert to domestic topics when confronted by a woman adept in nonstereotypical skills, and they didn't disappoint her; one of the first questions asked was if she could cook. Not satisfied with her affirmative answer, the reporters insisted on knowing her favorite dish. Jerrie has said in an account of that day that she was afraid the questioning about her domestic tendencies would overshadow the issue of women in space. Fortunately, the reporters seemed to get enough data about her recipes and moved on to more germane subjects.

Other news writers reporting from across the nation were not so gallant. One particularly gruesome diatribe published in the *Los Angeles Times* on August 28, 1960, was lengthy, but deserves highlighting for its malevolence toward any woman who would dare to step from the beaten path. In part it stated: "The scientists haven't even figured out how to get a man to the moon yet, but already they've opened the trip to women. That shows how far the craftier sex has come." It went on, saying, "Any beleaguered males who might have hoped that space would offer sanctuary from the war between the sexes must be disenchanted by the news that our space doctors are already screening women for the long voyage out and one healthy young lady has passed the test." The male author seemed incensed that women might prove better at space travel than men. "Certainly they can suffer physical immobility and subtle torture better than men. Most men feel imprisoned when they're in the barbershop chair. But women can spend afternoons under the hair drier. Any organism so placid and so easily amused should thrive on a mere 250,000-mile trip." His discourse continued on women's apparent ability to accept boredom. "They can abide excruciating boredom better than most men. Millions of them are content to spend years at the ironing board, soaking up the oleaginous oozings of the soap operas."

It was almost physically painful to read the continual venom spewed over the public at the thought that the final frontier was being invaded by women. Another editorialist droned on, "Most of the women with whom I have driven in automobiles would make admirable test pilots or anything since each sally forth is a fresh adventure. As for engineering, anything a woman can't fix with a hair-pin is unfixable by a corps of engineers."

Finally, as planned, in early September 1960 Jerrie's phase II testing was conducted under the auspices of the Veterans' Administration and the U.S. Navy at the Veterans Administration Hospital in Oklahoma City, including psychiatric and psychological testing. Because Jerrie wished to embark on this phase of testing in relative peace, she reported to work each morning to her job with Aero Commander, then participated in the tests each afternoon. After her brush with the press during the previous month, she was fearful they would hound her through this phase if they found out about it. The stress of dodging reporters might be enough to jeopardize the results of this all-important phase, so she developed this defensive strategy with her management. Testing included the Wechsler Adult Intelligence Scale, the Rorschach test, sentence completion tests, and the Minnesota Multiphasic Personality Inventory, as well as sensory deprivation testing, considered one of the most important tests of all.

The object of the test was to determine how susceptible a subject was to hallucinations with all senses deprived of input. Testing for the Mercury Seven astronaut candidates required a duration of only three hours in a darkened, padded air chamber, but Jerrie and all other women after her were tested in a new water chamber instead. Robbing its inhabitants of a sense of gravity since the water imparted a weightless sensation, the water chamber reportedly made isolation more complete than air testing.

Jerrie was deprived of light, touch, smell, taste, and hearing by being immersed into a specially constructed water chamber heated to match the exact temperature of her body. The chamber was located in a small room with steel walls eight inches thick; no sound, light, or vibration was allowed to reach her. She suited up, was lowered into the tank, and waited for hallucinations to begin. After several hours it's normal to "see" forms of light, but even though Jerrie remained in the tank for nine hours and forty minutes, she didn't report a single apparition. This was an all-time record until other women were tested. Reportedly, no one on the testing team was able to determine Jerrie's limitations to sensory deprivation. She said she enjoyed the experience and felt unconcerned for the entire time; she later admitted to taking a couple of naps. At the time Jerrie underwent testing, no one, man or woman, had remained in the isolation tank for more than six and a half hours without any ill effects.

Sensory deprivation experiments had proven resoundingly that women were more comfortable without sensory input than men, so Jerrie's results should have surprised no one. In November 1959, scientists in Canada had experimented with sensory deprivation with space travel in mind. They fashioned an isolation chamber consisting of a plastic dome in which subjects could stay "entombed" for days to determine reactions to the lack of sensory input. All of the men tested in this chamber had hallucinations in the forms of clouds and dancing lights. After six days of entombment, the first woman test subject showed no tendencies toward hallucinations, adding significant weight to the Canadian scientists' theory that women were superior to men under stress in general, but particularly under the stress of isolation.

The Canadian findings were augmented by simultaneous American research being done at the Air Force Aeronautical Laboratory at Wright Field, Ohio. Laboratory Director Colonel John Stapp said that men had not proven satisfactory subjects when testing for confinement and sensory deprivation; they were prone to undue worry about their families and becoming aggressive and irrational far too soon to embark on a long and confining interplanetary trip.

The British Interplanetary Society noted at a 1958 symposium on restricted environments that during experiments held in the mid-1950s, much the same results had surfaced: "For most of the isolation period the subjects displayed a curiously flat emotional state, interspersed with periods of mounting tension, restlessness and inability to sleep." Alternatively, a woman, Dr. Edith Bone, famous for having spent seven years in an underground isolation cell during World War II, seemed to have emerged without mental scars.

A sensory deprivation test conducted at the National Institute of Mental Health in Bethesda, Maryland, contained comments that "normal men, regardless of their motivations, could hardly stay both conscious and sane if deprived of all sensory stimuli beyond three hours." According to the study, scientists' concerns emanated from the results of their experiments that centered on evidence of impaired organized thinking and confusion.

The stress of confinement was of considerable concern to the scientists at NASA as well. NASA memorandum traffic indicated that they also questioned "man's" capability to endure stress caused by long-term confinement in a space suit. Terms used during discussions, such as "significant psychological stress," were linked to the requirement of wearing the suit for long periods. This was of such concern that this stress indicator was later used as a discriminator in the actual astronaut selection process. Termed "calibrated hazing," it included placing the astronaut candidates into stressful physical and mental situations and clocking their tolerance time, reactions, and degradation in performance. Predicted behavioral changes included unevenness in performance, increase of errors, loss of a normal level of proficiency doing physical tasks, and general confusion. Results from these studies indicate that women would perform far better during confining periods of space travel.

These previous experiments made the outcome of the phase II stress testing fairly predictable. The psychological, psychiatric, and isolation testing proved to be just as easy for Jerrie as the tests at the Lovelace Clinic. The write-up detailing results of the examination noted once again that Jerrie was capable of developing an immediate rapport with everyone involved. Dr. Kilgore of Lovelace had called it "ladylike" while Dr. Jay T. Shurley, professor of psychiatry and writer of the summary report of the tests done at the VA Hospital, noted how Jerrie charmed everyone, immediately establishing a warm and friendly accord. He wrote that her unfailingly pleasant personality was immediately noticeable. Dr. Shurley said he considered Jerrie to possess exceptional psychomotor skills and coordination and was impressed with an almost palpable single-minded pursuit of becoming an astronaut, so focused were her skills and mental ability. The report also said her piloting capabilities would hold her in good stead through all conditions, including hazardous ones. Along with a very high threshold for frustration, Jerrie had a personality, despite her intensity, that successfully charmed both genders. Highlighted in the report was her preference for action as opposed to inaction; but according to Shurley, she was easily able to withstand long hours of participating in nothing more than introspection, based on her sensory deprivation testing.

In summation, Dr. Shurley's final paragraph was unequivocal in his opinion of Jerrie and her capabilities. He noted no significant liabilities but thought Jerrie possessed "several exceptional, if not unique, qualities and capabilities for serving on special missions in astronautics, viewed from the standpoint of her personality makeup and functioning." He noted that she could be relied on both to give direction, if the task fell to her, or just as readily to take direction. He said she could remain observant, but relaxed, if no action seemed called for or an action might be detrimental. Dr. Shurley was very admiring of Jerrie's sense of self and motivation. Apparently, he believed he was assessing Jerrie for actual astronaut qualities, for in his final statement he wrote, "I believe she has very much to recommend her for selection as an astronaut candidate."

Bonding with the psychological testing team was quite different for Jerrie than it was for the men. Reports showed that the men being considered for the Mercury program were not happy about being subjected to psychological tests. They dreaded them and dragged their feet at every test. Despite efforts by NASA to soften the effects of the testing on the men, the NASA handlers finally reconciled themselves to the fact that there would always be antagonism between the test pilots and the evaluators.

The men had proven to be skittish of any tests, especially those without exact answers such as those used in psychiatry. In *The Right Stuff*, Tom Wolfe told of the consternation experienced by the test pilots during the psychological testing at Wright-Patterson Air Force Base during the Mercury selection process. "Military pilots, almost to a man, perceived psychiatry as a pseudo-science." What made it even worse was that none of the doctors running the tests for the Mercury program were impressed with the "test pilot" mystique most people felt in their presence: "To fighter jocks it was bad enough to have doctors of any sort as your final judges. To find psychologists and psychiatrists positioned above you in this manner was irritating in the extreme." The objectivity exhibited by the cadre of examining physicians seemed to offend the Mercury candidates. Complaints were often voiced that they were constantly looked at as though they were frogs or rabbits; they were just another type of lab animal.

Even though she was on cloud nine after her second successful round of tests, Jerrie continued her aviation life and took advantage of the downtime between phases of testing to do something she felt truly blessed to be able to do. She lived in an era in aviation where technology was advancing so rapidly that speed and altitude records were being set and reset regularly. Since she was such a superb pilot, Aero Commander arranged for her to attempt to establish a new altitude record in its latest two-engine propeller-driven airplane. This was a marketing ploy used by many of the general aviation manufacturers of the era, but Jerrie was still exhilarated at being allowed, no, requested to fly a beautiful machine so high up into the sky. On the appointed day, she rose early, ate a hamburger for breakfast, donned her equipment, and flew off into another record, returning to earth feeling joyous.

In the spring of 1961, her prowess and fame opened the door to another adventure when she flew the Goodyear blimp *Mayflower II*. Her reputation was so strong as a respected test pilot with fixed-wing aircraft, she was invited to take up the airship to give Goodyear her viewpoint on that type of flying. She enjoyed it enormously, amazed at the difference from "normal" flying.

After what seemed an eternity, Jerrie was invited to begin phase III of the astronaut testing process, conducted at the Navy School of Aviation Medicine in Pensacola, Florida. Few, if any other women had ever attended the Navy pilot testing facility and considerable curiosity was evident from the staff as to how she was going to fare. Her normal enthusiasm was without support; all of the men had a considerably different attitude from hers as they waited and watched, wanting to know if she could "cut it."

From May 15, 1961 at 8:00 A.M. until May 23, more than a full week, Jerrie's daily schedule was filled with tests, tests, and more tests. She was subjected to additional physiologic exams such as the oxygen consumption during grade change test, during which she walked on a treadmill at 3.5 mph with an 8.6 percent incline, striding for five minutes. She was allowed to rest for another five minutes, then returned to the treadmill at a harsher setting: 7 mph at an 8.6 percent incline. Since they have a naturally higher heart rate than men, comparable results for women in general and Jerrie in particular would have been even better if she had a naturally lower resting heart rate like the men who had been tested before her. Nonetheless, her score was well within the norm for a qualified man her age. After collapse, her recovery was measured and her score was calculated as a 44, considered within the average range for men of military age and fitness. She went through tests simulating artificial gravity, including a rotating room on a centrifuge, as well as a test simulating crash landings into water on a machine called a Dilbert Dunker.

Jerrie was trained in water survival techniques and ejection seat and airborne survival techniques, but her most "amazing" test occurred in a machine called a slow rotating room (SRR). A room fifteen feet in diameter with no windows, the SRR rotated, creating disorientation in the test subject. It had been developed several years previously to test aviators' reactions to certain types of motion. After entering the moving room and sitting momentarily, subjects are asked to accomplish specific motor tasks. Test objectives include showing the effects of the coriolis force on humans as well as inducing motion sickness. Most of the tasks are impossible to complete; the test results center on the severity of the candidate's reactions to the rotation, not the actual accomplishment of the tasks. Generally, both objectives, showing the effects of the coriolis force and inducing motion sickness, are accomplished. Jerrie remembers trying to hit a dartboard with several darts—made impossible by the rotation of the room. Reports showed her performance was good, comparing favorably with other experienced naval aviators, and with the advantage of being "markedly less hampered" by symptoms of motion sickness and disorientation than a group of incoming healthy male flight students.

The Dilbert Dunker, a mockup of an airplane cockpit, is small and cramped. Trainees are strapped into the cockpit, which is then set loose down a 45-degree rail to descend into a deep pool of water, turning upside down just before crashing to a stop. The water, shock of entry into a deadly environment, and inversion of the equipment serve to test the candidate's capability to react in an underwater emergency. Everyone who has ever seen the test or a depiction of it probably wonders how they would react if suddenly plunged into very deep water while tied to an inverted metal cage. This apparatus has been used to divide the "men from the boys" in thousands of training sessions for the military.

Jerrie embarked on the Dilbert Dunker test with a normal amount of trepidation. Determined to win this battle too, after she hit the water she very calmly and deliberately unlatched her seat belt; edged herself out of the cage even though she was wearing a bulky life preserver, clothing, and a full-sized parachute pack; and swam to the surface of the water seemingly unfazed.

The next test, even more complex, was the airborne electroencephalogram (EEG). Wired with EEG needles stuck to the head, the subject is strapped into a high-performance airplane. Results are recorded on instruments and a camera as the subject flies in a specially equipped airplane through a high-gravity load–stress aerobatic pattern. Eighteen needles stuck in Jerrie's head recorded her brain waves under unusual stresses, ensuring that any anomalies and reactions were noted to be later analyzed. The procedure was used to guarantee that each astronaut would be able to withstand similar stresses during any high–G force portions of the space missions.

Jerrie's riding in the Navy testing plane for the EEG required the Navy command in Pensacola to secure permission from Navy headquarters at the Pentagon. Detailed in the message was information

Jerrie Cobb in Air Force gear ready to take a ride. (courtesy Library of Congress)

that the flight was part of the testing to "ascertain the difference between men and women astronauts." In reply the Pentagon said, "If you don't know the difference [between men and women] already, we refuse to put money into the project."

Despite the wisecracks, the Pentagon higher-ups relented for reasons unknown and allowed Jerrie to take the airborne EEG. Maybe they were also curious as to the difference between men and women. All through the high-G turns and maneuvers, Jerrie's brain waves were recorded by the eighteen electrodes, and her physical reactions were noted with a movie camera. An ounce of vanity would have driven her from the screening room when she saw the film of her flight. Her face contorted and her eyes rolled, popped, and sank into the back of her head. These reactions were due only to the gravitational stress of the maneuvers and nothing else, so she passed the final test.

As Jerrie left Pensacola in late May, she was told she had done so well that all the other women qualified through the Lovelace Clinic testing would be allowed to go through phase III testing with the expectation that they would perform on a par with her.

Jerrie testified about all of this before Congress, calling to the sub-committee's attention that she had passed the same three phases of testing as the Mercury Seven men, pointing out that the men had gone on through the final technical training aspects of becoming astronauts whereas she had not been allowed to progress. Jerrie emphasized that no taxpayer money had been spent to support the women's room, board, or travel in preparation for each phase of the testing proce-dures. All the women had either paid their own way through the training and testing procedures or found someone who would pay for them. Today this would have brought tears of gratitude in Congress, but apparently it failed to impress the legislators of this earlier era.

Based on Jerrie's performance and the Navy's reassurances, the other twelve women believed that their inclusion in phases II and III testing was imminent. In fact, Rhea Allison and Wally Funk were invited to complete phase II testing at the Veterans Administration Hospital in Oklahoma City. Traveling to Oklahoma City during the same week of July 1961, they participated in the testing one after the other. Jerrie was so excited about the women's progress in the testing program that she asked them both to be her houseguests during this time. Her extra bedroom became the women astronauts' bunkhouse. Her excitement inspired her to decorate the bedroom with spaceship bedspreads and put celestial-print wallpaper on the ceiling. Charts of the solar system festooned the walls. She even coined the name "FLATS" for "first lady astronaut trainees," trying to give the thirteen of them some cohesiveness and identity.

A charter pilot and an instructor for an aviation company in Houston, Rhea flew to Oklahoma City in a Piper Comanche she bor-rowed from the company. She approached the tests in her own quiet way and completed them just as successfully as Jerrie had. Without dwelling on it, she and Dr. Shurley implied to Jerrie that she had done exceedingly well on the sensory deprivation tests, so well that she was very late to dinner at Jerrie's house that night.

Wally stormed through the phase I testing, during which she beat John Glenn's results on the stress and lung-power tests and also beat Wally Schirra's results on the vertigo test. She set a record in the bicycle endurance test while she was at it. By now, she was twenty-two years old and her fierce competitiveness compelled her to strive for even better results in phase II. During that series of tests, she endured the sensory deprivation portion of the testing for over ten hours and only came out when the testing personnel tired and ended the test. She was thrilled to have set a new record for endurance of sensory deprivation. When the week was over, Dr. Shurley noted to Jerrie, "You three share a common characteristic. You are all strong, silent women." When asked if that was a positive comment, he replied, "I only hope the rest of the group tests out the same way."

Because of the first three women's success, phase II testing seemed imminent for the trailing ten and for all twelve to follow Jerrie through phase III. As it turned out, because the three women who underwent psychological testing in Oklahoma City did so well, the testing personnel suggested that the final ten women go straight to Pensacola and begin the Navy's portion of the testing (phase III), forgoing phase II testing for the time being.

In May 1961, just days after completing phase III testing, Jerrie attended the NASA Conference on the Peaceful Uses of Space in Tulsa, Oklahoma, where many government and industry luminaries were in attendance. An evening conference banquet featured NASA Administrator James Webb as the speaker. His remarks caught Jerrie unaware as he noted her successful completion of all three phases of the testing. Then, without consulting Jerrie, he announced that he was naming her as a consultant to NASA. He stated how truly pleased he was to have access to Jerrie's input into the space program. In Jerrie's book, *Woman into Space,* she described her total shock at this announcement: "I couldn't believe it! Here was a bonus I'd never even contemplated. I was actually to have a say in America's move into space!"

A few weeks later, during a Washington, D.C. ceremony, she was sworn into the position. Another big step had been taken. She began the job full of hopes of influencing NASA's approach to the women's program. She had plans to help set up a program for women to test and train and become astronauts just like the Mercury Seven. She got busy and began drafting the plan and sending letters to all those who might be involved, soliciting input. Her first report was "a report that NASA wanted, and wanted pronto. Ideas on the why and how of women in space." The report, a two-part proposal, attacked dual subjects dear to her heart: "Part One was a recommendation that research be continued officially, by NASA, so women's potential contributions to space exploration could be thoroughly investigated and measured." The second part went to the meat of the issues the United States was facing in the space race: "Part Two was a plea that the first woman in space be an American, not a Russian. The Soviets had already racked up all the other firsts. Let this one be ours."

Even though she was unaware of any stir, Jerrie's performance during phase III testing, as well as her enthusiastic acceptance by the public as a speaker and consultant, must have set alarm bells to ringing in the halls of NASA. Her many nights on the "rubber chicken circuit," as she called it, giving speeches and raising the profile of the women's program, caused other women to be interested in becoming astronauts. A June 1961 letter written by G. Dale Smith, Assistant Director for Program Planning and Coordination, Office of Life Science Programs, to George Low, the NASA Director of Spacecraft and Flight Missions, addressed the importance of NASA's determining whether it was ready to accept women as astronauts. The document stated, "There are a number of letters being sent to Headquarters by women who wish to become astronauts. I hope you will have ideas on answering these letters. The medical portion of a selection and training program is but a guide in selecting physically and mentally qualified people, and as you know, women fall within the physically qualified, therefore, there must be other valid reasons why or why not we are to use women in our space flight program."

Phase III testing for the twelve remaining women was scheduled with the Navy for July 1961. As each woman struggled to fit this into her schedule, it soon became apparent that most of the professional women pilots were not going to be able to accommodate that date. Sara Gorelick Ratley was going to have to quit her job with AT&T, because it would not give her the time needed to participate in the tests. Another of the women, a flight instructor, was fired just for asking for time off, so the date was reset for September—September 18, 1961. Jerrie was uneasy about postponing the tests. In July, everyone on the Navy's side had been ready, but she had no option other than to wait for the new September date.

On September 15, less than three days before testing was to begin, Dr. Lovelace called Jerrie and broke the news that everything had been canceled by the Navy. She was crushed; some of the women were already en route. It fell to Jerrie to convey the devastating news to them as well as to weather her own disappointment and hurt. She told Dr. Lovelace that she would call Pensacola and determine the reason for the cancellation. He was not hopeful she would ever get a straight answer from the Navy brass, saying, "don't be too disappointed if it doesn't get you anywhere. There's never one answer or just one person involved in these things." Even though she was a consultant with NASA, she couldn't find anyone who would give her a consistent answer. Responses to her queries to NASA included, "Don't know," "What testing?" "Ask the Navy," "See NASA."

When she finally found someone in the Navy who would explain, she was told that NASA would not agree that tests on the women were needed. In a letter dated a few days later, October 2, 1961, Dr. Hugh Dryden of NASA confirmed to the Navy what had already evidently been discussed and decided among his staff about the women's program. "NASA does not at this time have a requirement for such a program. We do, of course, recognize that at some time in the future a decision to undertake studies of this nature might be made." This was a rather dry recognition that the inevitable inclusion of one distaff member into the astronaut ranks could, at this point, still be avoided.

Chapter Six

Even though the Pensacola tests had been cancelled, none of the women believed the fight was over. They all felt that sooner or later, NASA would realize what it and apparently the country already knew: The United States had only one "first" left and that was putting the first woman into space. Patriotism and pride compelled all the women to continue to wait, knowing they might be called on to undertake a role which was reserved only for the great and that their names could be forever emblazoned in the history books. They had been asked not to reveal their identities and they continued to abide by that request; besides, none of them knew the entire roster, for they had never been together as a group. They kept their hopes up and their stories silent for months, waiting for NASA to call them up and ask them to finish the testing that would launch them into astronaut training classes.

Jerrie wondered, at this point, what advantage her position as a NASA consultant had brought her. She had been stymied in her efforts to develop policies supporting women in space. She had been ignored by NASA management. She had ultimately been totally unaware until after Dr. Lovelace called her that the women's tests had been cancelled based on lack of support from NASA. She must have wondered why James Webb had even bothered to make the announcement. The only speculation that still has merit today is that Webb recognized the winds of the future blowing across the country (including the fact that women were becoming a constituency to be reckoned with) and thought that if the agency members appointed a high-profile woman, they would be perceived by Congress and the public as progressive managers who were living by the ethics of fairness.

Throughout all this time, the American public and the women astronaut candidates were well aware that the Russians were training at least one woman for another Russian space first. In an article published in *Town and Country* magazine, a Russian female scientist was very candid about her country's belief that women could do the job just as well as men and maintained that there were no differences between the training routines of the men and women. The thought that Russian women were being allowed to go freely through testing and competition for the right to become astronauts, must have been painful and frustrating for the American women—they couldn't even get permission to finish the tests, much less go through astronaut training.

Trying to overcome the logjam and get the testing started again in late 1961 and early 1962, Janie and Jerrie conferred with numerous government officials, including Lyndon Johnson, who at the time served not only as vice-president of the United States, but as chairman of the National Aeronautics and Space Council (the policy advisory group for NASA). They also contacted Congressman George P. Miller of the House space committee, and Congressman Victor Anfuso, also a member of the House space committee. Even though he was not vocal at this juncture, later on President Johnson was won over and gave his support to women astronauts when he said, "I see no reason why preparations should not be made for testing and training individuals who have the required physical and mental capabilities, regardless of sex." This was a whole new level of support and had it come in time, it might have given the women what they needed to break the barrier.

As Jerrie continued her report to the committee, she told of how all the women were so singular of mind that Sara Gorelick Ratley, who had a technical job at AT&T, had in fact quit when her astronaut training requirements began to take too much time. She was so determined to pass each test and become an astronaut that she sacrificed the significant start she had made in a technical career. K Cagle had postponed having her first child for a couple of years so she would be ready when the nation needed her. Each one of these women had paid her dues in one way or another in the field of aviation. They had had families, gotten degrees, and had flown an inordinate number of hours, gaining an impressive set of aviation credentials. Jerrie also recounted to the subcommittee some of the verbal abuse their dream had taken at the hands of the press.

Despite the efforts of all the women to maintain a low profile, she told Congress, inquiries began to filter in and break through the mantle of secrecy that had until now protected most of them from public pressure. As word leaked to the public that there were other women besides Jerrie being trained as astronauts, there began to be questions as to when they were to go into space and what their roles would be. Jerrie talked of the frustration they had all experienced when they were not taken seriously and that all during the time the women were in the testing phase, and even after the tests had been stopped and the program became public, how an enormous amount of ridicule had been heaped on the concept of women astronauts as well as these women personally; they had to endure the amused smiles of men as well as the barbs of both men and women.

Editorials abounded, amusingly discussing the problems women would have in space with floating nail polish, cookie crumbs, and bobbie pins. Personal letters were sent to NASA by women expressing a great deal of emotion about women astronauts. One, handwritten and sent directly to James Webb, was particularly emphatic. The author was unwavering in her opinion: "Keep the women out of the space flights. The damn crazy things. They would cause you a lot of trouble and expect special consideration and favors. The hell with them." These sentiments were the results of all types of motivation, including the idea that women, in general, were selfish, fractious, and incapable of understanding technical concepts. They may have also stemmed from the apparent divergence from the normal feminine graces to which most women were accustomed. The idea that women could be astronauts, with all the technical and mechanical expertise implied by the title, threatened many other women within their own lives of "normal" women's activities.

Oddly enough, this sentiment would pervade the modern space program and haunts women even today. During several *Mir* missions on which women were part of the crew, women crew members were criticized for not being feminine enough. Space history magazine, *Quest*, states, that mid-1990s Russian cosmonaut Svetlana Savaskaya was noted as being competent and capable, but "had a great deal of difficulty with her fellow cosmonauts on her first space voyage. The complaints apparently were that she was not feminine enough— either in looks, style of behavior, or in her interactions with them." United Kingdom cosmonaut Helen Sharman was ravaged for wanting to be regarded as a scientist and not a woman.

The press hadn't helped matters, either. Names such as Astrodolls, Astrotrix, Astronettes, and Space Gals were used with abandon. NASA did not even try to hide its disdain for the prospect of using women astronauts, and stated that it would much rather spend the money to orbit a "bunch of monkeys." Jerrie's measurements, to her horror, were published numerous times in the most popular national magazines.

Despite all this abuse, Jerrie noted to Congress that all thirteen of the women candidates had persevered. Besides having the right to make history, Jerrie explained, there were scientific reasons for letting women fly into space. "Without pretending to be either doctor or research scientist, I remind you that women weigh less and consume less food and oxygen than men, a very important point when every pound of humanity and the necessary life support systems is a grave obstacle in the cost and capability factors of manned space vehicles."

This was a reminder that payloads still had to be small so as not to over-whelm the boosting capacity of the U.S. rockets. The decade following World War II had been one of diverse scientific accomplishments by the two major superpowers. The Russians had spent the decade perfecting rocket motors that could push large payloads into space, and the United States had spent its time concentrating on long-range bombers. This left us without rockets large enough to counteract the Russians' accomplishments.

It was very expensive to place anything into orbit, so launching women could be crucial in saving significant amounts of money. Additionally, Jerrie discussed the intangibles that women could bring to space exploration. "Scientists say that women are less susceptible to monotony, loneliness, heat, cold, pain and noise than the opposite sex, vital facts to keep in mind in our nation's plans for space exploration of increasingly longer duration." Many of these factors would later be proven very advantageous to space travelers. When U.S. astronaut Shannon Lucid was dropped off at the doorstep of the *Mir* on March 22, 1996, she made history as the first woman to become a crew member on a space station. On September 26, 1996, when she was picked up by *Atlantis* space shuttle and brought back to earth, she not only became the woman with the longest time in outer space, she also became the U.S. astronaut with the longest time in outer space. She spent over six months in the space station and basically was none the worse for wear, either physically or psychologically. Despite the debilitating effects of space on the human body, Lucid was able to walk off the space shuttle under her own power, a feat that no one thought she would be able to accomplish.

Jerrie also pointed out to Chairman Anfuso that women have more finely tuned nerve reactions, required to execute delicate maneuvers such as those used in space travel. The Martin Company of Baltimore, Maryland, had provided simulated space flights under contract with NASA and had "found women had the edge on operating controls for space rendezvous." Later, during the Apollo program, as the United States readied for moon flights, some of the most critical concerns surrounded the ability of the astronauts to rendezvous the command/service module with the lunar module prior to departing earth orbit for the moon. Each of the two pieces of equipment was sent into space in a configuration demanded by the launch vehicle; then everything had to be unhooked from this configuration and rearranged into the final lunar flight configuration for the moon mission so that the lunar module would be properly positioned when the time came for the lunar excursion. It was an enormously delicate operation, and if the astronauts had not been able to execute this delicate maneuver millions of dollars and years of time would have gone down the drain. Based on the fine motor skills exhibited during the Martin Company study, having a woman astronaut to complete the effort could have made all the difference in smoothing some of the worries about the rendezvous process.

Continuing her testimony, Jerrie railed against the use of money in support of a colony of chimpanzees located at Holloman Air Force Base. They were being readied for space travel; she reasoned that if there was funding and support for sending these chimps into space, money could be spared to send women into space as well. Making the situation worse was the fact that four of the primates were female. In fact, on January 31, 1961, a chimpanzee named Ham had been sent into space and successfully returned to earth. The chimps had been trained to pull a series of levers and push buttons in a spacecraft after launch and were considered smart enough to get a free ride into space, yet despite their records, women couldn't find a way into the program.

Jerrie ended her testimony with a proposition, saying, "Women who want to be astronauts offer our flying experience, we offer thousands of flying hours over millions of miles, literally dozens of years, and experience in all types of aircraft, in lieu of the few hours of jet test pilot experience required by NASA." Jerrie then made the point that as of that date in 1962, despite overwhelming willingness, aptitude, and talent, there had been no women in space, and she fervently wished for that opportunity for one of the thirteen women who had begun the qualification process.

Janie was called to testify next. She immediately launched into the main premise of her speech: space had been turned into a men-only operation with active exclusion of women through a set of phony experiential requirements. "[I]t is inconceivable to me that the world of outer space should be restricted to men only, like some sort of stag club." She made the point that gratuitous inclusion of women was not what any of them wanted; they just wanted to compete on a level playing field for the chance to become astronauts. In one of the most compelling statements uttered over the two days of testimony, she said, "Let's face it; for many women the PTA just isn't enough."

Janie mentioned the expectations of more winks and knowing smiles, which all the women had endured (an unfortunate aspect of society experienced by women even today). She also mentioned the waste that the nation repeatedly created by assuming that women had nothing to offer in many fields, such as medicine and scientific research. When after significant periods of disbarment women had been allowed to contribute, enormous leaps in knowledge had been the result. She urged the representatives to open up this reservoir of talent and let it support space exploration.

After the women finished their formal statements, the critical issues were reexplored by committee members during a question-and-answer session. As Jerrie and Janie were quizzed, the subcommittee was told of the testing process the women had endured. All thirteen of them had been through phase I, three of them through phase II, and only one of them through phase III. Then Jerrie got to the crux of the issue. She noted that the requirements for consideration for astronaut training made it impossible for any woman in the United States to qualify at this point. These requirements included the following: each candidate should have at least 1,500 hours of jet flying time, be less than forty years of age, have a bachelor's degree in an engineering or scientific field, have graduated from a military test pilot school, and be less than five feet eleven inches in height.

The most unattainable of these requirements was that of being a test pilot. The basis for requiring graduation from military test pilot school reportedly revolved around the desire to keep out undesirable applicants and ensure that security was maintained. This was supposedly based on the background checks that had been performed on all the military test pilots (as though the same kind of checks could not be done on other applicants). It is widely believed that President Eisenhower created the final set of criteria for astronaut selection after discarding the much more liberal original ones, and that he in fact had exclusion on his mind when he created them. They proved to be so rigid and exclusionary that by the time the hearings were convened some had already been abandoned. (Subsequent to this time, most of the remaining original "Eisenhower" requirements were reconsidered and abandoned.) During the time that the original qualification requirements were in effect, the public and the thirteen women were told that the criteria were inviolate.

Despite this outward obfuscation, NASA went to great lengths to ensure that all the male astronaut candidates were told that the selection criteria, at some times, were allowed to change on a moment's notice. A checklist used at NASA around 1962 to prepare the personnel who briefed each new class of astronaut candidates stated clearly that everyone was supposed to make sure that the candidates knew "that firm standards cannot be established until further data [are] available." There was also an item that read "Have the astronaut candidates been apprised of the rationale behind the selection program and do they understand that standards in many cases are of necessity arbitrary?" A September 1962 staff report to the U.S. Committee on Aeronautical and Space Sciences pointed out that the tests taken by the men vying for a role in the Mercury program "were not a matter of passing or failing, but instead were [a] measure of how one candidate compared with all others." In fact, as noted earlier, when no other reason for trimming the candidate list for the Mercury program could be established, it finally came down to a very subjective determination of which ones "were real men." The privileges of inclusion using the flexibility implied by these statements were never afforded to anyone other than those chosen few who were influential enough to be exempted by the NASA hierarchy. If this level of wholesale exemption was the case for men, it should have also been so for women. The women maintained that if their tests and flying achievements had been judged without consideration of gender, several of them would have become astronauts. This flexibility was certainly never afforded the women. Worse yet, the Mercury astronaut evaluation process was not the airtight procedure that NASA said it was at this point. For example, the stress-testing portion of the Mercury program was conducted by the Air Force Research and Development Command under the watchful eye of Brigadier General Donald Flickinger. The general was serving as a member of the NASA Special Committee on Life Sciences. Since the physical stress of traveling to and from space presented the greatest risk to future astronauts, this portion of the evaluation process was of the highest importance during the testing phase. Despite its significance, a 1970 report discussing the stress-testing portion of the evaluation stated, "The Mercury candidate evaluation program, unfortunately, was to prove considerably less well structured than that envisaged by the U.S. Air Force because of time limitation, accelerated schedules, and the inevitable 'unforeseen changes'." In other words, many of the tests were hurried, changed to make them easier to complete, or recalibrated in some way so that the Mercury candidates could finish them more quickly.

Equally as interesting, the original job announcement promulgated on December 22, 1958, listed few of the final Mercury program requirements. It simply requested that anyone who wanted to become an astronaut respond to NASA. There was no mention of a test pilot requirement; just an applicant must prove that he or she had had "a substantial and significant amount of experience which has clearly demonstrated three required characteristics: (a) willingness to accept hazards comparable to those encountered in modern research airplane flights; (b) capacity to tolerate rigorous and severe environmental conditions; and (c) ability to react adequately under conditions of stress or emergency." The "job" categories that were considered when developing the original set of qualifications included balloonists, submariners, scuba divers (because of the use of specialized breathing equipment), mountain climbers, subarctic explorers, flight surgeons, physicists, astronomers, and meteorologists. Test piloting as proof of this qualification was used only as an example of fitness for the job, not set out as a prerequisite. If these requirements had been allowed to stand, not a single applicant would have to have been a test pilot. In December 1958, the job notice was advertised in the *Federal Register*. Almost immediately, it was cancelled and reissued with new and drastically changed requirements, including pilot as well as military test pilot requirements. Anyone who had been keeping score before the cancellation of the advertisement and after the reissue of the new announcement would have been mystified as to what had caused such a drastic change. Executive privilege had weighed in, however, and President Eisenhower's new modifications prevailed.

Many of the thirteen women applicants had worked as test pilots with propeller-driven airplanes, but had been excluded from being jet test pilots. As she testified that day in Congress, Jerrie reminded all present that being a jet test pilot in the United States in 1962 was the exclusive bastion of the male military pilot, because women in the military services were not allowed to fly jets. Therefore, they were not even considered for admission into either of the military's two test pilot schools. (The Navy's test pilot school is located at Patuxent, Maryland, and the Air Force test pilot school is located at Edwards Air

Force Base in California.) Jerrie lamented to Congress, "There are no other test pilot schools except those of the Navy and the Air Force and since there are no woman pilots in the services they do not have the opportunity to go to these schools to learn to be a jet test pilot or to fly in the latest supersonic jet fighter equipment either since they all belong to the military, and civilians are not allowed to fly them." She talked of friends from other countries, such as France, who were allowed to test-pilot jets without any concessions to their gender. The women of Russia had also been called on to perform what in this era were considered extraordinary aviation feats. During World War II, dire need had driven the Russian military to call for women pilots. At the height of the war, there were three air regiments the pilots of which were exclusively women; they were called the Night Witches. These three regiments were titled, equipped, and deployed operationally exactly as the men's regiments. The 586th Air Regiment was a defensive unit protecting communications and flying air cover for advancing Russian troops. The 587th Bomber Regiment was an offensive bombing unit. The 588th Air Regiment was the only one in which all personnel, from armorers to mechanics to pilots, were exclusively women. Members of the 586th had many confrontations with German pilots trying to destroy various Russian facilities. In one such altercation, pilot Valentina Petrochenkova was guarding a bridge against German bombers. One day while she and her partner were patrolling, a bomber appeared and began to line up for a bombing run on this strategic bridge. The women pilots immediately attacked. As they followed the bomber, Valentina recounted the action: "We got quite carried away by it all. We'd fire at him, climb and turn, and then dive back down on him."

Based on this groundbreaking utilization of women combat pilots in Russia, a common assumption made by all of those in the hearing room was that because there were Soviet women test pilots, and it was common knowledge that the Russians were racing to put a woman in space before the United States, that they were most undoubtedly grooming one of their female test pilots to be the first woman astronaut. This assumption proved to be very wrong. The first Russian woman to go into space, it turned out, couldn't even fly an airplane. But that event was still nearly a year away and as of now, the first-woman-into-space prize was still up for grabs.

Questions were still being asked of Jerrie and Janie by the subcommittee; they centered on why being a jet test pilot was or was not essential to being an astronaut. Jerrie discussed the great number of hours of flying time that each woman had, and explained that the amount of time in the pilot's seat can be as important as a test pilot's training because in her words, "Pilots with thousands of hours of flying time would not have lived so long without coping with emergencies calling for microsecond reactions." Without these reaction times, many of the women in the aspiring astronaut ranks would not have survived long enough to apply to become astronauts.

Overall, the average number of flying hours for the women astronaut trainees was much higher than that for the Mercury Seven. With an average airtime of approximately 4,500 hours, the women averaged nearly 1,000 hours more than the Mercury Seven men, who averaged around 3,500 hours. The major difference was the amount of time that each group had spent in jet aircraft. The women had none, whereas the men had an average of around 1,700 hours flying jets. This one issue was enough to cost the women any chance of being considered as astronaut material by NASA, even though some of the men had been given waivers on some of the other requirements.

The educational requirements originally set as criteria for choosing the Mercury Seven were not rigidly maintained. The requirement that each of the men have a college degree in engineering was not upheld in at least two cases. At the time of selection, neither John Glenn nor Scott Carpenter had degrees at all, but that requirement was waived so that they could become astronauts. Seven of the thirteen women had degrees including ones in math, physics, and chemistry; one even had a master's degree in mathematics. Supposedly, the waivers were granted because Mercury candidates Glenn and Carpenter were so superior in their physical aptitude that they were deemed to have overcome the need for higher education.

Carpenter had been a gymnast at the University of Colorado and had stayed in excellent condition during his military career. During the testing, the two men bested many of the previous scores earned on the physical aptitude tests. Tom Wolfe's book, *The Right Stuff*, explained the results of the tests: "Scott had broken five records in all, and Glenn was usually his runner-up." The doctors were astounded at the men's performance and wanted to "call Washington and tell them about these two guys." Wally Funk had beaten one of them on at least one of the physical aptitude tests.

Table of Women's Qualifications

Name	Degree	Engineering Degree	Flight Hours	Jet Hours
Jerrie Cobb	none	none	10,000	0
Janie Hart	none	none	2,000	0
Jan Dietrich	yes	none	8,000	0
Marion Dietrich	yes	none	1,500	0
Rhea Allison Woltman	yes	none	1,500	0
Irene Leverton	none	none	9,000	0
Bernice Steadman	none	none	8,000	0
Jean Hixson	yes/ master's (math)	none	4,500	0
Gene Nora Jessen Stumbough	yes	none	1,450	0
Jerri Sloane Truhill	none	none	1,200	0
Myrtle Cagle	none	none	4,300	0
Sara Gorelick Ratley	yes/math, physics	none	1,800	0
Mary Wallace Funk	yes	none	3,000	0

The number of flying hours that the top four women candidates had were impressive as well. Jerrie Cobb had over 10,000 hours, Jan Dietrich and Bernice Steadman had over 8,000 hours, and Irene Leverton had over 9,000 hours. The top three Mercury Seven astronauts had considerably fewer. John Glenn had over 5,000 hours, Alan Shepard had over 3,700 hours, and Deke Slayton had over 3,600 hours of flying time. Once again, the big difference was that considerable amounts of the men's time had been spent in jet aircraft. The women had chosen careers in aviation and devoted most of their young lives to flying. The Mercury Seven had been military officers for many years which included many duties other than flying.

Table of Men's Qualifications at Time of Selection

Name	Degree	Engineering Degree	Flight Hours	Jet Hours
Scott Carpenter	none	none	2,900	400
Gordon Cooper	yes	yes	2,600	1,600
John Glenn	none	none	5,100	1,600
Virgil Grissom	yes	yes	3,400	2,500
Walter Schirra	yes	yes	3,200	2,000
Alan Shepard	yes	none	3,700	1,800
Deke Slayton	yes	yes	3,600	2,200

As the testimony continued, the women were informed that keeping females out of danger was another reason they could not be allowed to venture into space. Scott Carpenter informed the subcommittee, "I think at this time it is definitely an experiment. There are many unknowns and it is important for us to eliminate as many of these unknowns before the flights [women's] take place as is possible." Carpenter had just completed his May 24, 1962, flight into space and must have understood just how many years his statement would bar women from space, because every time an astronaut was launched, it was clearly a very dangerous job. Jerrie and Janie were told that if anything went wrong and one of them was killed, it would be the end of the U.S. space program. NASA was apparently terrified that the public accord for the programs they were working on would turn on a dime at the first indication of trouble; they did not intend to take that risk by launching women into space. This was a narrow interpretation of NASA's collective fear of what might happen to the program if anyone was killed, not just a woman. It has been stated numerous times during the early stages of the space race that the death of *any* astronaut would have killed the program.

Death, it turned out, was not an overriding concern for the women. The Mercury Thirteen had come to the same reconciliation as most other pilots about death. They trusted their equipment and their skill. Death seemed to be an accepted copilot—one to watch very carefully—so that it never had the chance to take over the aircraft's controls. On the other hand, most of the male astronauts who spoke of their bargains with death believed that skill and cunning had little to do with meeting death in this space business. Deep down, finally, they believed that it came down to luck.

Despite NASA's intense concerns over the effect that the death of an astronaut would have on its program, it was sadly proven more than once that the deaths of astronauts, even women astronauts, would not stop the U.S. space program for long. During a testing session for *Apollo I* on January 27, 1967, three of the finest people the United States had to offer (astronauts Roger B. Chaffee, Virgil I. Grissom, and Edward H. White II) were killed in a command module that had never left the ground. After a day of never-ending tests in the command module, fire suddenly broke out inside the spacecraft. Within seconds the fire flashed and consumed the 100 percent oxygen atmosphere being used in the test. The astronauts sounded the alarm, but the hatch couldn't be opened in time. When Myrtle Cagle heard of the tragedy, she mourned the loss of these brave men. "I met Ed White," she would say later as she went on to name Grissom as one of her all-time heroes. (This accident and the ensuing investigation crippled and delayed the program for approximately eighteen months.)

The explosion of the space shuttle *Challenger* that occurred on January 28, 1986, involved the first death of a woman in the space program when both astronaut Judith Resnik and civilian teacher Christa McAuliffe were killed while launching into space. While the loss of the entire crew was an enormous tragedy for the families, the nation, and the space program, once again (despite dire predictions of consequences of a woman's death) the program was only delayed for investigation, retrospection, and correction, not canceled. Reportedly, at no point after either of the accidents were the entire space program and its accomplishments in danger of being dismantled. Too many positive features had emerged from the technological strides that were being made during the program for anyone to seriously believe that canceling it would have been good for the country. A worldwide satellite radio network was in the offing. Military reconnaissance was being done and the physical environment of the earth was being studied. The argument to eliminate the space program if a death occurred, which had been presented during the 1962 Congressional hearings, was proved to have been totally fallacious. (Other arguments considered convenient at the time were also later abandoned.)

Jerrie argued that equivalent experience between the two genders should be considered, and used John Glenn's educational waiver as an example. He, as well as NASA personnel, believed that his years of experience and exposure to complex engineering concepts made the education requirement a moot point; Jerrie argued that anyone who had 8,000 to 10,000 hours of flying could render the test pilot experience requirement moot as well. Recklessness is not in the makeup of any seasoned pilot, for that is the way they get to the point of their experience. Jerrie told the hearing, "I don't think the qualifications of an engineering degree and jet test pilot experience should just be knocked out, but NASA should realize there is an equivalent experience which we can offer."

When the committee put the question to John Glenn whether because he had been given a waiver on his lack of educational credentials the women should be given a pass as well, he unequivocally answered, "No." Congressman Fulton pressed the issue. "[O]n the basis of the requirements that Mr. Low has stated [college engineering degree], obviously Colonel Glenn would have been eliminated. You wouldn't have passed, because you don't have an engineering degree—do you?" After answering in the negative, Glenn insisted that he saw no compelling reason to give anyone else the same type of advantage that he had been given. Besides, as he noted that day, he had subsequently earned a degree.

To this day Janie remembers how some of the committee members seemed to be openly supportive and very positive toward the issue of women in space program. She had high hopes each time Representative Victor Anfuso from New York, as chairman of the subcommittee, helped bring out points that added to the overall weight of the case the women were trying to have considered. Representatives Joe Waggonner, Jr., from Louisiana and James Fulton from Pennsylvania both also asked questions designed to bring several favorable issues to light during the hearings. Representative Anfuso was very concerned to hear that the last phase of the tests had been canceled without warning only days before the women were packing to travel to Pensacola. On the first day, he promised to get an answer as to why the cancellations occurred from the NASA representatives, who were to testify on day two. Another part of the discussion revolved around how, if at all, to utilize women in the space program in the future. Everyone, including the women, maintained that their inclusion should not cause a delay in President Kennedy's goal of landing a man on the moon before the turn of the decade. Despite this goal, many people agreed that there was merit to considering how to add women to the program in some useful way.

Janie Hart proved to have amazing foresight when she expounded on her ideas of the eventual evolution of the space crew. She had an idea that flying into space would someday become a secondary part of the process, and she wanted to gain assurances that NASA would in the future add scientific personnel to each flight so that the pilot could tend to the spacecraft and the scientists could expend their energies on the data-gathering and observation requirements of each mission. Little could she know that components of this exact argument would rage within NASA for years, and that until *Apollo 17* was launched in December 1972 there was never a full-time scientist in space. (That flight was the first one on which a fully trained scientist who was a part-time astronaut was allowed to go into space and to the moon as a member of the crew.) Ultimately of course, the space shuttle has proven Janie correct in that the pilots take numerous scientists into space and their experiments are usually considered the most important part of the mission. At the time of the hearings, Janie also wanted the possibility of a woman becoming a scientific member of a space flight to serve as a beacon to young female college students who were interested in studying technical fields. This signaled her future devotion to causes that would create technical advantages for young women.

Jerrie held fast to her convictions that no matter the timing, women should be included in the current space program in all capacities and was emphatic on the point that they should not be shunted into a special "women's program." She wanted them to be allowed to be pilots. She believed that they should be added to training rosters and instructed until proficient; then they should be allowed onto the flight list ready to take their turn on a space flight. Obviously, many other people felt considerably different. To his credit, Congressman Fulton supported this viewpoint and even made the statement that women paid taxes in the United States and therefore should be allowed to at least use the test equipment located in Pensacola which Uncle Sam had bought with this tax money. He was in the minority, however. A *Washington Star* article seemed to sum up the majority feeling in the United States at the time: "To expose women, needlessly, to the known as well as the incalculable dangers of pioneer space flight would be like employing women as riveters, truck drivers, steel workers, or coal miners."

Chapter Seven

After Janie and Jerrie completed their first day of testimony, the committee turned to the famed aviatrix Jacqueline Cochran. Despite her early support for the program, they knew that she was no longer a friend of the Women in Space program. Janie had been invited to visit Jackie a few weeks earlier at her apartment in New York City. Hart had gone out of curiosity as well as with the hope of enlisting this very influential person firmly to the cause of the thirteen women in front of Congress. During the visit, Jackie told Janie that she was somewhat against the program's going forward. She indicated that she understood some of the problems that the Mercury Thirteen were faced with and felt it was not a good time to try to press the program into existence. She told Janie about how she had had to fight the military establishment when she headed the WASP organization to allow women pilots to fly during their monthly periods, and she thought the Mercury Thirteen's battle was going to be too hard to win and would hinge on equally foolish issues.

Based on what was considered lukewarm resistance a few weeks earlier, the vehemence of Jackie's testimony must have been a shock to both Jerrie and Janie who until that moment believed that she was not radically against the effort. As a matter of fact, Cochran had at one point provided unequivocal emotional and financial support to the testing program; however, her testimony before Congress was the opposite and mostly defended NASA and the exclusion of women from the astronaut program. Despite indications that the Eisenhower astronaut selection criteria were very definitely designed to exclude almost everyone in the United States at that time, Jackie testified, "I do not believe there has been any intentional or actual discrimination against women in the astronaut program to date." She went on to say that she based this opinion on how she had been treated during the course of her flying career.

This was a remarkably biased approach because, as a friend of President and Mrs. Roosevelt and the wife of a wealthy airplane manufacturer, she had had every conceivable door opened for her; no one dared to discriminate against her lest the offender hear from the president of the United States. But her words carried significant weight, because at this time she held more national and international speed, distance, and altitude records than any other person in the world.

She had been the guest of Colonel Chuck Yeager, who rose to international fame in early 1950 for his involvement in an endeavor called the X-1 program. This was a high-performance aircraft project headquartered at Edwards Air Force Base. It was actually in some ways the antecedent of the space program. Beautiful, sleek vessels that were seemingly a cross between an airplane and a rocket ship were created and flown to all sorts of new altitude and speed records. When Jackie decided to be the first woman to break the sound barrier in an airplane, she turned to Colonel Yeager. He not only provided her counsel, he flew a chase plane beside hers on May 18, 1953, when she realized her dream and broke the barrier.

She had been appointed as a special ambassador by President Eisenhower and she was also a lieutenant colonel in the U.S. Air Force Reserve. Anyone, woman or man, with these credentials would feel little sting of discrimination on a day-to-day basis, especially in the rarefied air of specialty aviation. She, in effect, did not live in the same world as the thirteen women who were everyday, working girls without the opportunity to develop the kind of network and credentials as had Cochran.

Cochran also testified that she believed that in a program as expensive and urgent as this one, no risks should be taken by using anyone who was not a proven test pilot with high-speed precision flying experience. She said that she felt that including anyone who needed years of additional specialized training would slow down the process or cost more money and would complicate reaching the national goal of landing a man on the moon. Jackie would have been astounded to learn that many years later, during the final stages of the race to the moon, the technicians who were responsible for readying the grossly complicated moon flight made it clear to the astronauts in training, despite their egos, that they could have taken an average person off the street and within a year taught him or her to fly to the moon; the electronic systems were so fully automated that very little flying ability was necessary.

Cochran also maintained that only the agencies directly involved with the space effort should have the right to determine who and what the astronauts' qualifications would be. This included only NASA at this point, so she was effectively telling Congress to "butt out." Based on her experience with the creation of the WASPs during World War II, she said that men and women would prove to be equal physically and mentally when subjected to the rigors of outer space, but that there was no proof of this at this point and it would be risky to try to prove it in the middle of the space program.

This seemed an odd point to make at such an early date in the space race. With only four American men having been into outer space at the time of the hearings (and these only for a matter of hours), it would be hard to prove with so little statistical data that men were any more capable of withstanding the stress than women. That was the point, of course, that the thirteen women were trying to get across. It was so early in the program that if they were included now, not only would valuable data be gathered regarding the differences between genders, but equal training and treatment might prove women to be just as good as men, or worse yet, even better.

Jackie had experienced an impoverished childhood in the lumber mill towns of the South. She began working at the age of seven because her family was very poor. By the time she was eight, she had a job in a cotton mill. In her book, *Jackie Cochran*, she recounts that she "worked twelve hours a night—from six in the evening until six in the morning." At the age of ten, she was supervising fifteen children, barely younger than she. Money became the only way out of this hand-to-mouth existence; this realization seemed throughout the rest of her life to have made her very wary of spending it on anything she perceived as frivolous. She repeatedly told Congress that the program was too expensive to allow the inclusion of women; this might drive costs up considerably due to additional training needs and attrition rates. Cochran even believed that marriage was a potential disqualification for the space program. She told the subcommittee, "I am thinking with the great rush that is necessary now to maybe catch up, from all I have been told by the newspapers, that we do not want to slow down our program and you are going to have to, of necessity, waste a great deal of money when you take a large group of women in, because you lose them through marriage." Four of the women trainees were already married, one with eight children, and they had not asked for any special exceptions to the training based on their status, but that didn't seem to mean anything to Cochran. She went on to explain that even though she had been on the board of directors of Northeast Airlines for fourteen years, she felt that training women as airline pilots was useless because of the cost and possible attrition based on marriage. She said that this was inevitable because, as she put it, "I think first and foremost no one is successful unless they are first a woman and first a man and have all of the instincts and desires of the two sexes." She also believed that extensive testing for women was called for, so that they could be proven worthy of the program; they should "put them through every single test as we know it now, short of orbiting." Oddly enough, that was exactly why the thirteen women had agreed to be tested, but when the results had been so positive, all tests had been stopped.

Cochran was ultimately forced to admit that even though it might be useful to have astronauts who were all graduates of test-flying schools and had engineering degrees, these requirements might not be mandatory. She pointed out that one of the greatest pilots in U.S. history had, in contradiction to NASA's assumptions of minimum education requirements, achieved only a high school diploma. Chuck Yeager, by this time in his career had attained the rank of colonel in the Air Force and was one of the most revered pilots in America based on his work with high-performance experimental aircraft for the military. His performance had not been impaired by the lack of a college degree.

When asked directly if there should be a crash effort to train an American woman to be the first woman in the world to fly in space, Cochran may have spoken the most truthful and prophetic words of all when she said, "I don't think it would justify having a crash program. It would make the hard years of training these men took look a little silly, even if it succeeded." That summation, coupled with an earlier comment from the committee (which had elicited laughter) saying that maybe the tests on the thirteen women had been canceled because the women were showing up the men, has never been proven, but the thought certainly is an interesting one. Maybe this banter was closer to the truth than anyone liked to admit.

Cochran chose to support women in general, but not the thirteen women whose futures were at stake. She was ever watchful to be sure the men were taken care of first. In a letter dated March 23, 1962, she wrote to Jerrie Cobb that during the post–World War II debate about whether women who had supported the American war effort should keep their jobs in the face of returning men, she had personally recommended that the WASP organization, in which women pilots had made such strides for women in flying, should be disbanded: "Otherwise the WASP might have become the subject of resentment by the male pilots." She seemed to be more worried about a backlash harming the reputation of the organization she had created than protecting the strides women had made into a world once owned exclusively by men.

During the hearings, she maintained that the women's space program should start over from the beginning with a much larger group (150 to 200 women) and that these women should be young. She felt that when marriage was in the offing, women would not be able to devote enough time to keeping up with the fundamental training requirements, much less the special requirements of astronauting, even though her own history belied every part of this statement. When Congressman Fulton pressed her on her statement that marriage should be a disqualifier, she finally relented. Based on the fact the all the Mercury Seven were married, that could not be a reasonable exclusion.

The question of opening the military academies to women to serve as training grounds for becoming test pilots and then astronauts was also discussed with a great deal of emotion. This route would have ensured that women could become jet test pilots; Representative Fulton suggested that maybe the academies should be opened to women immediately so that the same training process would be available to both genders.

Cochran was horrified at the audacity of even proposing this notion. She said, "I don't think you should open the Academy to women. Maybe never. You have the ROTC, NROTC, perhaps institutions of higher learning in which you can put them. Don't clutter up the Air Academy with women unless we know we want them."

She and others helped to ensure that this kind of "clutter" was only allowed to happen when the Air Force Academy was finally opened to women over a decade later, in 1976. Even though this took place after Jackie quit flying in 1972, there is no indication that she ever changed her mind. Fortunately, for many of the women astronauts to come later, this exclusion crumbled just in time to put them in the front running to join NASA after graduation from one of the academies.

"Modern" women astronauts have the excellent training ground of the academies to thank for their outstanding performance. Astronauts Susan Helms graduated from the Air Force Academy, while Wendy Lawrence, Kathryn Hire, Lisa Nowak, and Sunita Williams came from the U.S. Naval Academy. Commander Lawrence was to ultimately distinguish herself in her conduct during what could have been another public relations disaster for NASA. Commander Hire is notable in that she conducted airborne oceanographic research missions all over the world in a specially configured P-3 aircraft. She went on to become a flight instructor in T-43 aircraft, but this was to occur many years after this July 1962 day.

As the first day of hearings wound down, Jerrie and Janie felt that they had made their points and were somewhat optimistic about the results.

Chapter Eight

On Wednesday, July 18, the hearings continued with the testimony of two of the highly revered U.S. citizens of the 1960s, Navy Commander Scott Carpenter and Marine Colonel John Glenn. On February 20, 1962, John Glenn had been the first American astronaut to orbit the earth. His ride lasted four hours and fifty-five minutes. On May 24 of the same year, Scott Carpenter had taken virtually the same ride; his mission had lasted one minute longer than Glenn's. These flights were only months old and a few hours long, but these two men were considered the most experienced astronauts in the country and therefore most qualified to testify at these hearings.

So with them and other witnesses, the second day of testimony began. As the hearings commenced, it was very apparent that the subcommittee members were starstruck. Of the four Americans who had ventured into outer space as of this date, two of them were sitting in this hearing room. Unrestrained with their opening comments and praise, the committee introduced the astronauts as "Americans of heroic stature." No less starstruck were they when later they introduced "the new breed of American, the space scientist" George M. Low, the Director of Spacecraft and Flight Missions in the Office of Manned Space Flight of NASA. Low had worked his way up through the early years of the U.S. space program after earning two degrees in aeronautical engineering from Rensselaer Polytechnic Institute, had been one of three men who made up the NASA astronaut selection committee when choosing the Mercury Seven, and was considered an expert on the requirements for astronaut selection.

Low began his testimony with the news that NASA had recruited a new class of astronauts and the final successful candidates were in the process of being screened. These new astronauts were to train for the Gemini program—the program including a two-person spacecraft that, as it turned out, was used mostly as a testing and training platform for tasks to be accomplished prior to the United States completion of the moon landing program within the Kennedy-prescribed time frame. The new qualifications by which this class of astronauts had been judged were significantly different than the ones used to select the Mercury Seven group. The age requirement had been revised downward so that now successful candidates could be no older than thirty-five years. The height qualification was raised by an inch to six feet. A degree was still required, but now it could be in one of the sciences as well as in engineering. Most significant, the original requirement of 1,500 hours of jet experience had been changed; this generation of astronauts need only be jet test pilots which could be achieved through both the military and NASA. While this opened up the qualification process to civilians, it was still a very limiting factor for all U.S. women, because women were not allowed to fly jets in the military (and it was not likely that NASA was going to let them learn to fly jets in their test pilot program either).

John Glenn was called on to give a statement, and he made the point that it was adaptability and reliability that made human presence critical in ensuring that our space endeavors were successful. "He brings to it his judgment, and not only the judgment from his training, but also the judgment that he brings to the program from his past background and experience," he said. If an emergency occurs, "the astronauts' function is actually then to take over full control, to analyze, assess, and report the various things that he encounters." If there is human presence, the adaptability of the human brain will ensure

that all measures that can be taken will be taken to support the success of the mission. For this reason, Glenn believed that having a test
pilot background was essential to becoming an astronaut. He failed to
mention that many of the Mercury Seven had taken a considerable
hiatus from the test pilot atmosphere during their time as astronauts;
at one point, the astronauts even had trouble maintaining a minimum
level of flying proficiency (four hours per month) in any aircraft
because of their busy schedules and the lack of available airplanes at
NASA. The *Washington Star* reported that there were morale problems in the group for many months after they were chosen. One of
the astronauts was quoted as saying, "We were brought into this project because of our proficiency in high-performance aircraft. Now we
can't get any time in high-performance planes." This fact notwith-
standing, Glenn maintained that the majority of critical in-flight
astronaut situations would be similar to those which test pilots had
gone through and could not be duplicated through other experiences.

Despite testimony from Glenn that piloting a spacecraft was an
arduous and hair-raising experience that required split-second
eye/hand coordination, astronaut Gordon Cooper described a considerably more serene scenario in a *Life* magazine article in which he
wrote, "He will use his manual controls to tilt the capsule into position for firing the retro-rockets, hold it steady while the rockets fire,
flip the capsule back into position for re-entering the earth atmosphere, and monitor the controls during re-entry to make sure the
capsule stays on an even keel." (This was confirmed with a check of
the early design philosophy used at NASA.)

There was a feeling that because the ability of humans to function
in space was an unknown, as many of the processes as possible in
the space capsule should be automated. The human was to ride along
as a passenger and observe. Even later, when the missions and the
equipment were made complex enough to take people to the moon,
it was a given that there was very little flying to be done, just a lot of

riding. In Andrew Chaikin's book *A Man on the Moon,* Frank Borman admitted that "the real role of the commander on these missions wasn't to fly the spacecraft; there was precious little of that." *The Right Stuff* author Tom Wolfe put it rather more bluntly: "Astronaut meant '*star voyage*' but in fact the poor devil would be a guinea pig for the study of the effects of weightlessness on the body and the central nervous system. The astronaut would not be expected to *do* anything; he only had to be able to take it."

The original description of the duties of the Mercury Seven astronauts developed in 1958 stated that the first duty of the astronaut was to "survive." Additionally, the argument that the men who flew were special because of their test pilot training was a shaky one at best, because even the men who became astronauts had deep concerns about whether they were there to pilot or to ride the *Mercury* capsules. Chaikin's book, *A Man on the Moon,* also quotes Pete Conrad, who attempted to qualify as one of the original Mercury Seven and later qualified in the second class of astronauts, as being relieved when he was passed over the first time. He believed NASA was looking for people who were in excellent physical condition rather than excellent pilots. The lack of need for piloting skills indicated to him and other astronaut wannabes that there was probably very little flying required, just stamina to withstand whatever happened to you after you blasted off. (This idea was called "the man in the can.") Reportedly, even the Mercury Seven had doubts that they would be pilots, but rather because of the regimented processes the *Mercury* flights had to go through, would just be passengers. Deke Slayton was to write a study a few years later that defined the Mercury program as just a step toward the "real thing" of space travel: "Project Mercury was simply the first peacetime step in the long journey of space exploration ahead, a journey that would proceed at whatever pace ever-advancing technology coupled with scientific research and development permitted," something to be endured until the real action began.

During these moments of the testimony, the consensus was that only women who had extraordinary qualifications might be able to qualify as test pilots, and women trained at that level might be very hard to find. Glenn testified, "I think perhaps at present it is a little premature to introduce them into our manned space program unless we could find the extraordinary one who is qualified as a test pilot." This was said knowing that three of the best women pilots in the country and maybe the world were an arm's length away, and also knowing that not a single one would be allowed into test pilot school. It was said also with the full knowledge that the Mercury testing had been developed with a scattershot approach that included anything that the scientists could think up, because they had no idea what forces would interact with the mind and body once the astronaut was in outer space. It was clearly understood almost from the beginning that this testing was a hit-or-miss process because no one had ever objectively been able to determine what kind of testing would be adequate for men or for women.

This was another infuriating and demeaning experience that Jerrie and Janie had to endure. Their logbooks would have proven that between them they had far more hours of flying time than the two astronauts. An additional indicator of the era in which the impossible was being attempted was that during most of the testimony and conversation, all references to people within the space program were made in the male gender. Each time there was a reference to future astronauts or engineers, it was in the male gender until the subcommittee chairperson finally made a note of it. It seemed as though no one in the room except Jerrie and Janie could fathom an engineer or a test pilot or an astronaut as anything other than a male.

Outside the room, the attitude was the same. Despite the fact that the subject being discussed on Capitol Hill by this subcommittee was of national importance, the newspaper coverage was lukewarm. The *Washington Post* devoted approximately six inches of space to the story and instead of placing it in the front section of the paper, placed it in the women's section. It was 1962 and still deeply into the unenlightened era for this country with regard to the equality of the sexes. Worse yet, very little backlash had occurred against this attitude; there were no women's rights activists available to help set the record straight.

As the testimony continued, it became apparent that because there were enough men available, women would probably never be needed as astronauts. In his testimony, George Low made it very clear that this endeavor was far too exclusive to allow women to partake. "We don't foresee in the near future—talking about the next five or ten years now—the need, at any given time, for more than perhaps forty or fifty space pilots in the NASA program. We see, therefore, at this time, no need to broaden out the available pool of people that we could use as test pilots." His premise was proven correct in that it was over fifteen years before the first women were ever "needed" and allowed to enter the astronaut corps, and another five before one went into space.

Low provided another flawed argument when discussing the training requirements of women. He maintained that if women were allowed into the program, it would disrupt the training schedule of the other astronauts. At this point, there were only seven astronauts; one has to wonder how much time they could spend on the training equipment. Besides, the Mercury Seven training program had been designed to be conducted "on an informal basis" according to a Senate staff report to the Committee on Aeronautical and Space Sciences. Another reason that women could not be spared the time could have revolved around the fact that others were using the training and testing equipment in addition to the Mercury Seven. Although it was not publicized much at the time, at least one additional person who was not in the ranks of the Mercury Seven was being allowed to use the training equipment—the astronauts' personal physician, William K. Douglas, a doctor, flight surgeon, and lieutenant colonel in the Air Force, was joining most of the testing and training at will. Even though it was not essential to his work, he patterned each day in the same way as the astronauts to familiarize himself with the testing process. He was in every true sense of the word the eighth astronaut.

Even with the addition of the next class of astronaut trainees (who had entered the selection process on April 18, 1962), it could not have been too crowded. When they came on board in September after final selection, the nine in the second class added to the six remaining in the first class (Deke Slayton had been taken out of the Mercury Seven rotation due to a medical problem) meant that there were only fifteen astronauts in training. Low must have had difficulty using this as an argument, but he said that to allow women onto the training equipment, much less into the corps, "would be interfering with the current program" to a very high degree. Such use would jeopardize the entire space program for the men. He said this also knowing that the new, huge manned spacecraft facility in Houston, Texas, was just months away from its September 12, 1962, dedication and that the availability of this facility would add significant training venues to NASA's stable. The lack of training facilities was to become the watchword for years in the concerted effort to exclude women. Anytime someone pushed the issue of including women into the astronaut corps, the response would be that women were welcome, but that it would delay the program and jeopardize the mission to the moon, which President Kennedy had proclaimed vital. Brandishing this admonishment was always enough of a threat to ensure that the encroacher would retreat and that the program remained strictly male.

George Low also had very strict opinions about whether numerous flying hours could compensate for the test pilot requirement. During the previous day's testimony by both Jerrie and Janie, they had highlighted that three of the women trainees had an inordinate number of hours in the sky and that this should supersede the need to be a test pilot. Low fiercely opposed this idea. He maintained that men had the capacity to react calmly to emergency situations and without this calmness, which they theoretically learned at test pilot school, missions would be placed in harm's way. His implication was that no woman could possibly function in the type of emergency situations that were likely to face the astronauts. When asked, astronauts Carpenter and Glenn basically agreed with this assessment.

Jerrie had had many close calls based on circumstance and not carelessness, and thought of these experiences as the testimony continued. There was the time she had agreed to pilot a company plane full of press to Washington, D.C., for the Kennedy inauguration. As her airplane, full of passengers, approached the District of Columbia area, an unexpected storm turned each area airport into an impossible ice bed, forcing her to circle for hours waiting for a break in the clouds that would allow her to use one of the airports. After approaching and being waved off at different times at the three local airports, matters were becoming desperate. Her wings were icing and the situation became critical. Finally, even though the airport was officially closed, air traffic control at Washington National broke its silence and began to talk the planeload of frightened reporters down from the sky. Fuel was so low that Jerrie knew they had only one go at landing. At four hundred feet, they still could not see the runway lights. She wasn't totally sure there was a runway in front of them, but she had no choice other than to go downward through the slush and fog. Finally, the lights pierced the heavy gloom and there was the runway and the emergency equipment waiting for them. Fourteen inches of snow greeted them on the runway. They had only six gallons of fuel left. Their airplane was the only one that landed at Washington National Airport that night in total blizzard conditions; a less talented pilot never would have made it.

Fortunately for the future of the space program, the opinion of women's lack of skill in an emergency was not shared by all of Low's peers. Many experts of the era felt that women might make much better astronauts than men, including the previously mentioned Colonel John P. Stapp, director of the Aeronautical Medical Laboratory at Wright-Patterson Air Force Base, Ohio, who maintained that a woman "would make an ideal space traveler." His tests showed that men were apt to worry about exterior things too much to be able to maintain a calm demeanor on a long, confining space trip. Unfortunately, none of the people with this frame of mind were asked to testify, nor were they in a position to sway NASA for the benefit of the thirteen women.

Later that day, the hearings became more patronizing toward Jerrie and Janie. As the conversation turned to possible timing of when women might be allowed to enter the astronaut corps, Mercury Seven astronaut Scott Carpenter spoke up, voicing concerns about the unknowns of space travel and the need to make it safe before women were allowed to partake. As Carpenter put it, "We're protecting the space program" by not allowing women into any unsafe situations, thereby ensuring there were no unwanted diversions from the program and the mission if one of the women were injured or killed. When talking about the timing of allowing women into the space program, Commander Carpenter gave Congressman Fulton this answer: "There are many unknowns and it is important for us to eliminate as many of these unknowns before the flights [women's] take place as is possible."

This statement totally disregarded the fact that women were sentient beings with the capability of preparing for this all-volunteer program. It discounted their intelligence, indicating that maybe they could not make up their minds without help from men. Congressman Fulton seemed to understand this implication and was fully unimpressed with that answer asking, "Doesn't that lead you into the old question of protecting women? And to me it sounds as if we are going to protect women in the kitchen, on the ground, and in the home. We do not want them to get out where things are exciting, or have adventure, where there might be risks."

If women had had to wait for inclusion until space travel was made perfectly safe, women would not be in the program even today, because space travel, like air travel and auto travel, may never be completely safe. Congressman Fulton once again proved to be the most plainly spoken in his defense of allowing women to participate. (Even forty years later, Janie Hart remembers his dogged sense of fairness toward them.) Despite opposition from the committee, who wanted to hurry to completion, he insisted on having his say and challenged the guest speakers as well as the subcommittee leadership on their inaction. He wanted to have women involved in the process immediately. In referring to the fact that Jerrie had been made a consultant for NASA in a never-defined, never-consulted position, he said, "To me it just seems arbitrary at this point to shunt them aside and say, 'You are a consultant.' "

Congressman Fulton then went so far as to recommend that the United States begin an official "first woman in space" program, which was envisioned as a parallel training program allowing women to catch up with the men and then go into space in a professional capacity. This idea was greeted with enthusiasm among the subcommittee members, but noticeably less interest from the NASA personnel. George Low was very unhappy with the prospect of anything that might slow down his program, and immediately began to rally against it with a predictable approach: "It would slow it [the moon landing] down in that all of the resources that we have available—and I can only speak for the manned space flight program now—are required for projects Gemini and Apollo. If we diverted some of these resources, both financial and personnel, to another program, we would necessarily have to slow down our national goal of landing a man on the moon before the end of this decade."

It seemed once again that when the status quo of the all-male program was challenged, the threat of missing the man-on-the-moon date was waved like a flag as a good reason to exclude women. In fairness to Low, he was reputedly a man with a singular ambition—putting a man on the moon before the decade was complete, but it was as though allowing a single woman to even enter the training program poised the sword of failure over the very soul of the space program. One has to wonder, if the moon shot were not in the offing, what would the next excuse have been for excluding women from the program? Ultimately, when pressed for an answer as to why the women's testing had been canceled, Low told the hearing that if NASA had any need for women, and there were any qualified ones, he would allow them to be tested. Currently, he stated there was no need because the Mercury Seven were available and even if he had the need, there were no women who could qualify. Despite the fact that the NASA job announcement dated December 22, 1958, clearly stated that all candidates must be males, he concluded with a denial that there had ever been any intention of creating a bias in the astronaut corps.

The ultimate artifice in arguing the point against adding women to NASA's astronaut rosters was then revealed when the potential cost of training the thirteen women was broached. This portion of the argument was probably one that sent shivers into the very heart of each subcommittee member; the thought of the need for more money for the space program was frightening to politicians because by this time in 1962, hundreds of millions of dollars had already been rerouted from other pressing national programs, such as the war in Vietnam and the War on Poverty, into NASA. Responding to a question from Ohio Congressman Walter Moeller, George Low probably drove a proverbial wooden stake into the heart of the program by announcing that it would cost more money to train women because "the training program would have to be far more extensive, and because there are no women today who are up to the same level of background as there are men." He also assured the subcommittee that costly adjustments would have to be made to various pieces of equipment, including the pressure suit and the space capsule itself. In fact, costly adjustments had to be made to each capsule based on its mission, and even more to the pressure suit. Each astronaut's suit was custom built to fit his physique as well as to fit the objective of the mission. A different mission objective meant that a different suit was needed to comply with the requirements for training, evaluation, or development.

Today's suits are manufactured so that almost any physique can be accommodated. The components, upper torso, lower torso, arms, and gloves are made in different proportions so that a suit for almost any physical size can be combined from production-level parts for a safe fit. (This process has been found to be much more cost effective than the previous system, in which each suit was custom built for each astronaut.)

When on day two of the testimony, one of the two women on the subcommittee finally spoke up, Congresswoman Jessica Weis of New York began to press Low about what she recognized as the obvious, built-in bias in the selection criteria against women. She discussed with him the dichotomy contained in the part of his argument in which he stated that women could become test pilots if they were interested enough, and added that in her opinion, "definite road-blocks" were apparent. When Low ducked the question and passed it to Glenn and Carpenter, the answer that came from Colonel Glenn may have summed up the entire feeling of NASA and all the men from that era. He said, "I think this gets back to the way our social order is organized, really. It is just a fact. The men go off and fight the wars and fly the airplanes and come back and help design and build and test them. The fact that women are not in this field is a fact of our social order." Embodied within this one thought was a national sentiment that would prove difficult for women to overcome for many years yet. It gave men, in all walks of life, an immediate argument as to why things were the way they were and why they shouldn't change. It was the reason women were not allowed to vote until well into the twentieth century and has been used as the reason for almost every other roadblock ever placed in front of strong and ambitious women. Even as late as 1998, when questioned about it Glenn still maintained that the statement was correct for the times.

There were apparently, according to all documentation researched for this book, no opposing opinions for years to come from anyone at NASA or the astronaut corps. Many agreed, including Frank Borman, who provided his philosophy on the subject of women as astronauts, which included the fact that during the initial experimental stages it would have been "silly" to have allowed women to participate. Yet he agreed that later, when space exploration became more mundane and astronauts became like "bus drivers," he thought women might be able to qualify.

As the next topic unfolded during the hearing, the irony of the conversation would not be totally realized until early 1998, a full thirty-six years after the conversation was held in that hearing room on Capitol Hill. As the concerns of potential discrimination against other populations were more fully explored, there was a concern that maybe by changing the candidate age requirement from forty years to thirty-five years, possible age discrimination would result and lead to one more factor which would continue to discriminate against women. To the question of eliminating the age factor completely, Low replied, "at this time, and for this selection, the best advice we could get, medical and otherwise, tells us that as people get older there is a greater chance of them either having to drop out during the training program, or even becoming incapacitated during flight." Today, in an era in which age has little relevance to accomplishment, this conversation seems a little ridiculous, but in the light that one of the people in that hearing room, who at least tacitly agreed with that statement, is now a seventy-something astronaut who has, as of October 29, 1998, returned to space aboard the shuttle flight STS-95, the conversation seems totally outlandish.

In the end it seemed that even those subcommittee members who were sympathetic to the thirteen women took John Glenn's reasoning as an easy way out of having anything constructive come out of the hearings. Congressman Waggonner from Louisiana tied everything up for the participants nicely when he said, "I think Colonel Glenn has hit in his statement on the exact differences of opinion which exist here, and fundamentally our social order prescribes some differences. This program is developed to this point because of the differences in our social order which time has laid down for us."

Congressman Waggonner invoked a particularly "Catch 22" type of argument as to why women could not become astronauts. He said that because none could qualify, that none were qualified, therefore none could be astronauts. Congressman Anfuso agreed: "We don't have any women candidates to do the things that these astronauts can do, and for that reason, they are disqualified at the present." Congressman Moeller agreed by asking the "good ladies to be patient and let us get things [presumably the moon landing] accomplished first." And so the committee members lined up to shake Glenn's hand and get his autograph and the women knew they had lost.

Even though subcommittee chairman Anfuso directed George Low to return to NASA and consider creating at least a parallel program with the goal of qualifying women to go into space, it is apparent that he was ignored. In the rest of the world, things continued as usual. A 1973 article in a popular magazine discussing the women space candidates talked about some of the comments made to the press during the time of the Congressional hearings. It notes the 1962 comments of a NASA spokesperson as saying, "The talk of an American space woman makes me sick to my stomach." Others went on to confide that they had enough problems with the space program without having to think about women. They were saved from this problem for many more years.

According to Congressional records, the subcommittee hearings had been scheduled to continue into the next day, July 19, 1962, so that summations could be given. As the second day's hearings were adjourned, Janie and Jerrie were bewildered and mystified when the chairman noted that this was the final day and that the hearings on this subject were concluded; they were not prepared for this; they had closing testimony that they had wanted to present. As a poor substitute, they were allowed to provide written summations for the record and these were added to the testimony, but it is fair to say that they and the transcribers who worked for the congressional recording service were probably the only ones who ever read their summary thoughts.

The presence of some of the data which had been added for the record at the end of the session transcript brought out during the course of doing research for this book was a surprise to the women who were most affected by it. None of those interviewed were aware that Jacqueline Cochran had added for the record comments that implied that Jerrie and Janie were mavericks and did not represent the entire group of thirteen women. She wrote, "I question that any person who expresses contrary views [to those Cochran had already provided] has been appointed or drafted as spokesman for the eleven not present at these hearings." In 1999, Ms. Hart denied that they were acting outside the group and was surprised to hear of the charge.

After the hearings, through sheer force of will, testing went on in bits and pieces, but soon even that little bit of momentum was lost. According to Rhea Allison Woltman, she had been scheduled to go to Pensacola for phase III testing in 1963, "but the Russians launched Valentina Tereshkova and that was it." The Tereshkova launch trashed any additional hope that women in America may have held out toward establishing a women's program or including a woman in the mainstream astronaut program.

Chapter Nine

In June 1963, Valentina Tereshkova of the U.S.S.R. blasted off in *Vostok 6* to become the first woman to fly in outer space. Her voyage was not unexpected and therefore was met with a series of antipropaganda sound and media bites from the West's men-only bastion. Almost to a man, they maintained that the flight was a public relations stunt and that it was for romantic "man-in-the-moon" reasons that the

Wally Funk (sitting, facing camera, third from right) attending a meeting with Valentina Tereshkova (standing) in 1990. (courtesy Wally Funk)

Russians had even bothered. Although it is hard to say where he got his information, Astronaut John Swigert, Jr., was particularly vocal about Tereshkova's flight, saying that she had been terrified during the mission and had not contributed anything other than to ride along. One has to wonder where his insider information was coming from. It was true, she was not a pilot; that didn't seem to make any difference in her ability to become an astronaut, however. She was an accomplished parachutist and since certain scenarios during the Russian recovery process demanded that the astronaut be experienced with a parachute, this may have been the most critical criteria in her selection. The *New York Times* thought that one plausible explanation for Valentina's success as a cosmonaut was that "any well-coordinated person, male or female, can be trained to perform what is required on a space mission." Her record-making ride was considered by American women as validation of the edgy beginning of their quest to become equal with men in the space race. The *Times* article continued to a conclusion about the American program which the thirteen women would have welcomed a few months before: "This country's apparent emphasis on the need for the professional test pilot is somewhat misleading." The Communists were given credit for permanently breaking the men-only barrier of space travel; this was considered proof that at least one superpower believed that women had the same virtues as men, including bravery and intelligence. Others thought that the Tereshkova flight highlighted the inadequacy of the United States to fully utilize its advantages.

Russian women reportedly danced in the streets when the news was released that Valentina had been launched into space on that June day. The Mercury Thirteen women were not dancing in the streets; in fact, as she remembered the events leading up to Tereshkova's launch, Jerri Truhill said in a 1995 interview in the *New York Times*, "We could have been the first person to put a woman in space and back then we really needed a first. We could have done it,

but the guys didn't want us." B. Steadman reflected the disappointment, saying, "We thoroughly expected at that point that we would
be accepted into the NASA program. We were told that. When we
were first asked to volunteer, it was a 'possible.' When we got to
Albuquerque there was no 'possible.' It was going to happen."

There was ignorance about the thirteen women's quest, as well.
Instead of celebrating the readiness of the American women and
insisting that they be added to the astronaut roster, there was snide
denigration of their willingness as a whole to step up and be counted.
In response to Tereshkova's flight, Senator Ernest Gruening from
Alaska was ruthless: "In entrusting a twenty-six-year-old girl with a
cosmonaut mission, the Soviet Union has given its women unmistak-
able proof that it believes them to possess these same virtues. The
flight of Valentina Tereshkova is, consequently, symbolic of the eman-
cipation of the Communist woman. It symbolizes to Russian women
that they actively share (not passively bask, like American women) in
the glory of conquering space."

But instead of being totally devastated that none of the American
women trainees were going to be first into space, the original thirteen
women believed that Tereshkova's journey into space would be a
brickbat with which to hit NASA and make it come around. After their
initial disappointment, the women were reportedly exhilarated by her
feat. Jerrie was particularly hopeful, saying, "Now, maybe we'll get
some action." Years later Jerrie and Valentina met at the Federacion
Aeronautique Internationale meeting in Mexico City, where the two
women and Russian astronaut Yuri Gagarin were being honored for
their early 1960s aviation and space records. During one of the many
long discussions among the three of them, Jerrie was startled when
Valentina asked her why she had not been first into space since she
had been "in training for three years" before the Russian woman's
flight. It had been a given in the Soviet Union that Jerrie Cobb was
going to be the first woman to break the gender barrier in space.

Jerrie's fame in the United States had been fleeting, but in Russia, she had been picked as a person with talent worth watching.

The thirteen women did not achieve the goal they had set out for themselves, but they paved the way for some extraordinary changes for women in the United States.

NASA and the public slowly began to come to grips with the idea of women in space, but not gracefully. Just a few short years after the hearings, the addition of women to space flights was being openly discussed. Many doctors associated with the space program were wrestling with the problem of extended space flights and how to make men more comfortable through the long months of travel to our sister planets. One of the solutions being discussed was the addition of women to the crews for recreational sex. Chuck Berry, from NASA, addressed a space medicine conference in late 1972 and broached the subject quite openly reporting, "For long-duration flights such as Mars, the crews would be confined inside their spacecraft for nearly a year. With so much time on their hands, they'd react like other normal human beings, they'd want sexual diversion." He finished his comments with a belated reassurance that of course these women would be "fully operational crew member[s] not only there for sex." There were also the inevitable discussions of how two different genders could coexist in the tiny space capsules. While speaking on the subject of women, Walton L. Jones, who specialized in the life sciences at NASA, said, "They'd certainly complicate things because there's quite a moral question involved that would have to be overcome."

Others had different ideas regarding the possible problems if women were allowed into the program. An Air Force research scientist stated that maybe women would be physiologically better suited for space than men but that mixing the sexes was just asking for trouble. "There's just too much difference between men and women. We really don't speak the same language. Imagine putting them together for that long. We'd be creating a communications problem that could be avoided." Once again, the concept of sentience in a woman was missing.

The thirteen women's contemporaries proved to be some of their harshest critics when asked about women going into space. Comments included those of the 1964 winner of the Powder Puff Derby (a women's national aviation competition), Mary Ann Noah, who responded to the thought of women astronauts with, "I hate to be a traitor to my sex, but I do think men can go it alone in this field for a while." Worse yet, Noah's copilot, Mary Aikens, added, "This country feels protective toward women and leaves it to the men to do the pioneering."

Women continued to apply to become astronauts, but each received the same answer. One woman, a space physicist commented after being rejected by NASA that what the screening board was obviously looking for was "Jackie Kennedy with a Ph.D." By the time the second round of astronaut selection was completed in September 1962, the requirements had changed, just as George Low had said they would. The requirement to be in the military had been abolished, the educational requirements had been broadened to include specialties other than engineering (such as physical or biological sciences), and test pilots were given preference, but the required number of flying hours was reduced and civilians as well as military pilots were eligible. The September 1962 group of nine astronauts did, in fact, include two civilians. By the time the third and fourth astronaut classes were selected, NASA began to recruit with academic qualifications in mind. By the June 1963 date on which NASA issued the call for the third class of astronauts, the requirement for flight experience was relaxed still further: 1,000 hours of jet time could substitute for test pilot certification. Soon, the call went out for less perfect bodies and more perfect and inquiring scientific minds in those wishing to become astronauts. A government adviser on space biology wrote, "In selecting the ideal humans to conduct experiments in space, we should place greater emphasis on the qualities of imagination and general intelligence and informedness as opposed to the narrowly specialized trainee."

As all of this unfolded, others continued damning the shortsightedness of the NASA officials. After the Tereshkova flight, an editorial appeared in the Newport News *Times Herald*. "'Tis sad but true that the U.S. space project people dropped the ball in the space game when it turned down women to the program more than a year ago. Had they been accepted, the distaff members of our society would too be able to leap off into space now to reap valuable scientific information. It would have also upped the prestige of this country in the vital space race." The editorial continued by concluding that if this is the best the best thinkers can come up with, women might not get to space at all. By June 1965, an entire class of astronauts was chosen based on not knowing how to fly at all, but on being scientists. Once again, it was an all-male class.

Today's qualifications for capturing a spot on a shuttle crew vary widely, based on the type of position for which one is qualifying. Applications are accepted on a continual basis; civilians may apply at any time while military personnel must apply through their respective commands for nomination. There are three different major job designations for a shuttle crew. The pilot astronaut can function as either the commander or the pilot of the shuttle. There is a requirement of 1,000 hours of pilot time in jet aircraft with flight test experience listed as "highly desirable" for these personnel. The mission specialists are basically experts in the complex systems used on the shuttle; they also must have in-depth knowledge of the operation of the supporting equipment used for the experiments conducted on each flight. The payload specialists are not astronauts per se but people who have the credentials to fill unique requirements based on a specific mission of a particular shuttle. They could be nominated by a company whose experiments are part of the shuttle payload and who have great in-depth knowledge about that experiment, or be a representative of another country who is flying as a goodwill partner or to take some shared experience back to his or her home country. They are not part of the astronaut candidate program, but must have an education level commensurate with the needs of the experiment. All successful candidates must meet physical standards of various levels depending on the position.

This devolution (regressive evolution of the astronauts' mission from flying to scientific endeavor) of the astronaut qualifications has indeed changed the perspective of what space travel is really about. It has rightly become more about science than glory and flying. The terminology has changed from space flight to space exploration. The astronauts are important during the transportation process, but it is the scientists who carry the knowledge and tools from which we gather most of the value from our forays into space.

Chapter Ten

The women rode off into the setting sun without experiencing any of the glory nor the achievements they had dreamed of for many years. Some were angry and some were disappointed. Jerri Truhill said in a 1991 interview in the *Dayton Daily News* that in the end, "We were denied it simply because we were women. And to this day, I absolutely resent the hell out of it." She went on to say that some of the women's lives as well as their careers had been destroyed because of these events. They had almost been a part of something so important that it is considered as one of the defining moments in the world's history, but at the last minute it had been swatted away from their reach. Most of them felt as though they had been deprived of something. The feeling was captured for that era of women when Betty Friedan characterized the problem of the country not taking women seriously as a national issue: "The problem that has no name—which is simply the fact that women are, kept from growing to their full capacities—is taking a far greater toll on the physical and mental health of our country than any known disease." Some of the thirteen women, though, were very philosophical about the entire effort, and as one put it, "A one week physical exam was not the highlight of my life." Despite any lingering trauma, they have all without exception subsequently lived very full lives.

Jerrie Cobb has, until recently, shunned the spotlight on this subject. She is still beautiful and the signature blond ponytail is still in place. She became a missionary to the indigenous tribes in South America located throughout the Amazon River basin, flying food and medicine into the region for church groups. She brings passengers, doctors, medicines, clothing, and seeds. Her days are hazardous; she flies without conventional navigation aides, just by the seat of her pants. Most of her constituents are of another world; some have not yet even discovered the wheel. She was deep in this other world when she learned via her airplane radio that astronauts Neil Armstrong and Buzz Aldrin had landed on the moon. It was as if the two worlds existed on different planets. She wished them well and went back to her work.

For one who has spent most of her time out of the limelight, Jerrie has received an amazing number of recognitions. Honored by the governments of Ecuador, France, Brazil, and Peru for her humanitarian use of the aviation prowess she possesses, she was also honored by President Nixon at a White House ceremony for her achievements as a pilot. In 1981 she was nominated for the Nobel Peace Prize for her enormous contribution to the people in the Amazon River basin. The nomination put Jerrie in the company of some legendary personalities and international achievers. In spite of all her notoriety, she continues flying professionally and has amassed over 55,000 hours of flying time. When she learned that John Glenn had wrangled a return flight to space in order to study the aging body, she was finally prompted to return to America and campaign for her shot into space. Glenn had spent many years as a U.S. Senator representing Ohio and had used his last bit of influence to talk NASA into a last ride for himself. Jerrie hoped for his help in her own endeavor, but never heard from him. There is no indication why Glenn did not respond, but this particular subject seems to be difficult for him to consider. He has maintained from the beginning that he got a bum rap when people accused him of stifling the women's program, and he has consistently shied away from speaking about the entire subject.

In October 1991, Jerrie and Irene Leverton caught up on a lifetime of experiences when they both attended the thirtieth reunion staged for the thirteen women at the International Women's Air and Space Museum in Ohio. Irene had devoted her life to being a professional aviator and now has over 25,000 hours of flight time. She says that as she looks back on that life, she realizes how hard it has been to stay true to her original love of flying professionally, but has decided that it was the right life for her. In retrospect, it must be difficult to look back on a life of sacrifice and wonder to what end your sacrifices have brought you. She says, "I had to give up many things over the years to be a pilot." But she continues, "I was always looking for adventure." Sometimes when adventure couldn't find her, she made life into an adventure. When she was asked to join the Women in Space program, she was flying for an air taxi company located in Southern California. She needed time off to go to Albuquerque for the tests, but the company refused to allow her to excuse herself; she lost the job. Skeptical all the way, she recounts her reaction when told the women were not going to become astronauts: "I'll tell you exactly what I said when I heard we weren't going to Pensacola, 'So, what else is new?'" She was subsequently a crop duster pilot, a corporate pilot, and a check pilot for a Japanese airline school based in the United States.

Irene Leverton in 1995. (courtesy Michael Althaus)

The experience she considers the most fun was when she flew contract work and was chosen to transport U.S. Forest Service personnel into one of the national parks in the Sierra Nevada Mountains. Oftentimes, this included flying the fire boss over the latest forest fire for reconnaissance work. She has devoted her life pushing forward the concept of women in the field of aviation. She founded the Women Pilots Pylon Racing Association in 1964 and the Women's Airline Transport Pilots Association in 1969. She has said that she began the latter organization just so that the public would be exposed to women pilots and realize that it was just as natural for women to fly an airplane as it was for men. She continues learning and has attained flight and instructor certificates for single-engine land and sea, multiengine land and sea, commercial instrument, gliders, and Air Transport Pilot. Irene became an FAA designated pilot examiner and from 1981 until 1995 she was the examiner at seven U.S. airports. Even though she is over seventy years old, she is still a member of the Civil Air Patrol (CAP) with the rank of captain, and is involved whenever needed in search and rescue operations within her patrol's area of responsibility. She is proud that she is still able to respond to call-for-emergency flights for Squadron 205 of the Arizona CAP. In her spare time, she flies part-time for one company, while owning her own aviation service business called Aviation Resource Management in Arizona.

Marion Dietrich continued her writing career; she became quite successful writing for such publications as *Time* magazine. Marion is one of the two women from the group who is deceased. Her sister, Jan, continued flying as a corporate jet pilot. Reportedly the Dietrich twins were being considered from afar by NASA as candidates to fill one of the two-man space missions for the *Gemini* series of spacecraft on the drawing board for launch after the *Mercury* series had been completed. Based on their weight and smaller requirements for food and oxygen, Marion and Jan could have saved the space program tens of thousands of dollars compared to the two men who flew the same mission (not to mention the advantage of physiologic studies on identical twins in space). After Marion's death, Jan fell into ill health and has never recovered.

K Cagle was also at the thirtieth reunion and regaled all of the attendees with stories about becoming an airframe and power plant mechanic for the Air Force. She is still an instructor and a Civil Air Patrol pilot. After the reunion, she spent several years before retirement in 1996 working as a C-130 aircraft propeller mechanic at Robins Air Force Base in Georgia. She has never ceased in her criticism of the way NASA overlooked women's potential contributions. At another of the women's reunions at NASA for the February 1995 launch of Eileen Collins's flight, Cagle still hadn't forgiven the men who had robbed her of her dream, commenting, "Most of us had more flying time than those jockeys did," referring to the Mercury Seven men.

Gene Nora Stumbough Jessen was forced into looking for what turned out to be her dream job, after quitting her position teaching at the University of Oklahoma in order to journey to Pensacola for the phase III testing. Days after she was replaced, she was notified that the tests had been cancelled. Her job unrecoverable, she landed another job flying Beech Aircraft products in Wichita, Kansas. It was a placement that was her ideal; in addition, she met and married her dream man while at this job.

She and her husband later owned a Beech Aircraft dealership while he continued to build a business as an aviation insurance specialist, all while living in Boise, Idaho. They raised two children in Boise and have recently owned a fixed-base operation there. Gene Nora is still an active pilot

Gene Nora Jessen in 2001 readying to take off. (courtesy Gene Nora Jessen)

and has served as the national president of the women's aviation organization, "The 99s." When Shannon Lucid was chosen for the astronaut corps, one of Gene Nora's former flying students called her and with great excitement explained that he had been Lucid's flight instructor. Since Gene Nora had been his instructor, he felt that Gene Nora was Lucid's aviation grandmother. Jessen is still very proud of the Mercury Thirteen's contributions to the space race. When discussing all the women who had become astronauts since the Mercury Thirteen had gone through testing, she said "Our timing was wrong, but I think we paved the way."

Wally Funk joined several of the women at the 1995 reunion at NASA and told how she continued to try to get into the all-male bastion at NASA and, of course, continued to apply for the astronaut program. She evidently tried to break down the doors of the training facilities as well. In late 1962, as part of an effort to round out her space dossier, she arranged to be tested in the centrifuge and take the

Mercury Thirteen at the February 1995 launch of Eileen Collins first flight as shuttle pilot. Right to left: Gene Nora Jessen, Wally Funk, Jerrie Cobb, Jerri Truhill, Sarah Ratley, K Cagle, and B Steadman. (courtesy NASA)

Wally Funk teaching a student how to plan an airplane race in 1973. (courtesy Wally Funk)

U.S. Marine high-altitude chamber tests. She was unrelenting in her pursuit of a place in NASA's lineup and ultimately applied to become an astronaut four times (the last in 1970). That time NASA may have considered her application seriously, for she was told that if she could earn her engineering degree within the next twelve months, they would allow her to begin training. Needless to say, she didn't have a chance of attaining a degree within that time frame and walked away totally heartbroken that her finest and most long-standing dream was never to be.

Wally then redoubled her efforts to stay near her first love, aviation, and went on to excel in another all-male field, the Federal Aviation Administration (FAA). She was the first female General Aviation Operations Inspector ever to be hired by the FAA. After several years there, she moved her career to the National Transportation Safety Board (NTSB), the organization responsible for investigating all air crashes (as well as other transportation mishaps) to determine their cause and promulgate any policy adjustments which should be made in order to keep a particular kind of air crash from happening again. She was the first female Air Safety Investigator for that organization. After ten years of service with the NTSB, Wally retired and went on the lecture circuit, disseminating her knowledge about the causes of airplane crashes and possible preventive measures that could be implemented to stop them.

In a *Los Angeles Times* article dated July 19, 1962, Wally vowed never to give up the fight and predicted that one day she would go into space. She has never let go of her dream and is still looking to hitch a ride; she is vying to be one of the first commercial passengers on regularly scheduled space flights and hopes to go into space in the year 2004. She is as excited as a child about this prospect and about what she will see when she arrives in space for the first time: "I'll have my nose pressed against the window, enjoying that view."

After the Pensacola tests were cancelled, Janie Hart continued the life that she and Senator Phil Hart had begun and raised their eight children; along the way, however, she was very active in the national political scene. She became an antiwar activist during the Vietnam War. Her idea of civic duty is to protest what one does not like, so she actively protested the war. One day she joined hundreds of protestors as they invaded the Pentagon for a prayer vigil. All of them were arrested on what Janie calls bogus charges because the only thing they were guilty of was "praying in an area of the Pentagon that was set aside for prayer." Large buses were brought to one of the Pentagon's doors and they were all herded on and taken off to jail. They were charged with disrupting the operation of the Pentagon, which turned out to be a misdemeanor. Even though it was a minor charge, she was required to be present during a trial at the nearest federal district court. On the appointed date, she was totally unprepared for the press response to her court appearance. When comparing the press coverage of the women astronaut hearings to that she received at the courthouse in Alexandria, Virginia, she said there was no comparison; she was swamped when she went to court. It saddened her to know that a little civil disobedience could garner so much more publicity than the hearings on women in space.

Janie has come to recognize that even though she was not allowed to go into space for the nation, the public profile she gained as part of the effort was a springboard from which she was able to figuratively fly and do so much to help the women's movement. Subsequent to the hearings and much to her surprise, one day out of the blue she received a call from Betty Friedan, the famous women's liberation activist. Friedan was calling to say that she had heard of Janie during the astronaut hearings and wanted her to become one of the founding members of the board of directors for the National Organization for Women (NOW). Needless to say, Janie agreed.

Another opportunity presented itself when, based on her new and higher profile, she got a call from Liz Carpenter, representing President Lyndon Johnson and asking her to lead a women's advisory group for the FAA. The president said he wanted this group up and running within a week. Even Janie was not one to argue with the president of the United States, so she called on several friends for help; among them they were able to contact enough talented women aviators to create an advisory group within the deadline. It was called the Women's Advisory Committee on Aviation. Fran Bera, who was one of the original twenty-four Lovelace test subjects that had missed the cut for the Mercury Thirteen, delighted Janie by agreeing to join the group.

Janie led the committee, ultimately providing the FAA with numerous issues that should be addressed for the good of all pilots. The committee members suggested the development of such programs as parallel runways at the busiest airports in the nation to facilitate faster and safer handling of arriving and departing aircraft. They also foresaw the need for the general upgrading of the air traffic system to support the burgeoning aviation interests in the United States. (The upgrade of the air traffic system is still being addressed today by the FAA as part of the National Airspace System program.) The committee insisted that the FAA ban the practice by airports of requiring women to pay to use the rest room, whereas the men were not charged. While a seemingly small issue, Janie recalled many an airplane trip that ended as she shifted from foot to foot while she and Phil stood outside the women's room and pooled their pocket money for the correct change for her to open the rest room stall door.

These were all-important tasks for the good of the nation, but when asked what was the most important and long-lasting effect of her stint as an astronaut-in-waiting, Janie recently told a story that Phil had recounted to her many years earlier. A few months after her new, higher profile had taken her into NOW and the country had begun taking the women's movement seriously, Phil said that he began to notice a difference at his committee hearings. Prior to the formation of the women's movement, when his committee was scheduled to discuss "women's issues" most of the members would find other things to do that were "more important" than the hearings. After the perception of U.S. women began changing through the highlighting of the Mercury Thirteen and activities supported by NOW, on days when the committee was to hear women's issues, the seats would be full.

Even though today Janie is at the age where some women might tend to slow down a little (nearly eighty) she doesn't show any signs of looking for that proverbial rocking chair. In the mid-1990s she helped crew a large sailboat from Spain to the British Virgin Islands, saying, "Out there [on the ocean] no one can tell me what to do." She now spends part of each year living in Michigan, where she can be near a lake and go sailing any time she wants. She still loves Washington, D.C. for its fall and springtime weather and the friends she left behind, but she is happiest when she is on the water in the

Jerri Truhill in early 1960s. (courtesy Jerri Truhill)

Caribbean sailing. Hart also said that if for any reason she was asked to go into space, she was sure she could pass the physical and would be ready at a moment's notice.

Another of the women who has regretted her circumstances enormously, but never allowed them to stop her from achieving, is Jerri Truhill. When approached to volunteer she remembers her reaction as, "[G]ee, they can't even get a rocket off the launch pad. They keep blowing up, and they're talking about astronauts." She was very disappointed never to go into space, but she continued to build her flying skills as well as her business. One of her most exciting experiences was when she was flying on contract as a test pilot for Texas Instruments and had a chance to flight-test several new pieces of highly secret spy equipment. One of these was the prototype of the terrain avoidance radar, whose progeny was proven to be of lifesaving value for American aviators during the Gulf War. She also tested a prototype infrared detection system that was the first device to photograph and prove that indeed Castro had missiles in Cuba, thereby precipitating the Cuban Missile Crisis. She flew B-25s, B-26s, and DC-3s. She started her own aviation business; at one point she added a male partner as an expedient method of ensuring that government contracting officers did not overlook her woman-owned business when handing out contracts. She had no plans to fall in love, but that partner, Joe Truhill, later became her partner for life. When she finally had time to slow down, she served on the board of directors of the International Women's Air and Space Museum located in Ohio.

Rhea Allison Woltman lives in Colorado, where she folded her wings shortly after the tests were cancelled and became a professional registered parliamentarian. She reveled in each renewed friendship during the Mercury Thirteen's thirtieth-year reunion sponsored by the International Women's Air and Space Museum in Centerville, Ohio. It had been years since she had seen Jerrie Cobb, B Steadman, K Cagle, or Irene Leverton. The dedication that Rhea and the others continue to have concerning the legacy of the Mercury Thirteen was deeply demonstrated when Jerrie Cobb told of the extremes she had endured just to get to the reunion. She had begun five days before, traveling in a dugout canoe. After her trip downriver to an area populous enough to have an airport, she had taken a series of small airplanes until she reached Bogota, Columbia, and had then taken a series of larger commercial planes until finally reaching Ohio.

Still a cheerleader for the effort, B Steadman has worked hard to keep the story of women in aviation and space alive by becoming one of the founders of the International Women's Air and Space Museum. She is currently on its board of directors, for which she has served as president and chairperson. She owned an aviation business in Michigan for many years while also sailing the Great Lakes. She recently added her voice to those lamenting America's lack of foresight in not launching a woman first. "We were there, we were ready, we were motivated; the space program has always been something that has brought the world together to deliberately miss that opportunity I thought was bad for my country." Steadman and her husband currently own a business not related to aviation in upstate Michigan.

Sara Gorelick Ratley probably suffered the greatest loss when she gave up her professional technical career at AT&T to ready herself for the astronaut training at Pensacola. After the effort was not successful, she chose not to return to her original career and retooled her talent from engineering to accounting. She worked in her family's accounting business to begin with, then branched out to own her own company. She busily took accounting courses and ultimately passed the examination to become a certified public accountant. She is now a CPA living in the Kansas City, Missouri, area. She still flies for the joy of it and, she like all the others, would be willing to go into space anytime NASA wants her.

Jean Hixson became a teacher in Akron, Ohio, where she spent thirty years. She was in the Air Force reserves for many years, and in 1982 retired from that organization as a full colonel. She subsequently succumbed to cancer. According to Jerri Truhill, Jean was the smart one, and with her advanced degree in mathematics would have been a very great asset to NASA.

Dr. Randy Lovelace, Jr., was an extremely dynamic and intelligent individual. As one of the foremost thinkers in the world on aviation medicine, he had several inventions to his credit, including the original oxygen mask used in high-altitude flying. According to his associates at the clinic, Lovelace knew everyone who was remotely involved in the business of space. He and Donald Flickinger were very close, and after the Mercury Seven had completed their tests at Lovelace, he was quite close to many of them as well. In 1965 he became involved in a Colorado think tank called the Aspen Institute of Humanistics. After one of their regular meetings in Aspen, Randy, his wife, and their pilot decided to fly a shortcut over the Rocky Mountains back to Albuquerque. Through a navigational error, they turned their airplane up the wrong canyon—one which turned out to be a box canyon—and crashed into the canyon wall. After three days, rescuers finally arrived at the crash site. There were indications that one of the passengers had lived long enough to leave footprints around the destroyed fuselage of the airplane, but it was December and whoever had survived the crash had succumbed to the cold before the rescuers arrived. Randy's death was a great loss to the aviation community and many friends, including some of the Mercury Seven paid their respects at his funeral.

Jacqueline Cochran continued her flamboyant ways for many years. One of the people interviewed for this book said that Jackie never entered a room without making sure that everyone noticed her. They continued to notice her as she kept on flying for any record she could find, including becoming the first woman to fly a jet across the Atlantic Ocean. But even she could not last forever; in the 1970s, when she was over sixty years old, she began to have fainting spells which effectively ended her flying career. She had a pacemaker installed to regulate her heartbeat and she and her husband retired to their southern California ranch and lived together until his death in 1976. She continued to decline until her death in 1980.

Many a young female heart had been set to fluttering and mind to whirling at the thought of becoming an astronaut, and despite all the disappointments the women were dealt and all the demeaning talk of curling their hair and doing their nails in space, one of the most striking things, which was discussed repeatedly in all of the sources was the reverence with which each candidate approached the thought of becoming an astronaut. Jerrie Cobb noted it, and Marion Dietrich discussed it by calling it the "greatest honor possible." They all intuitively understood that everything they might do would have a lasting impact not only on themselves, but on everyone who was to follow behind them, especially those who were to follow immediately.

In an article written by Clare Boothe Luce for *Life* magazine in June 1963, she wrote from the heart and with an understanding of the era, saying, "The astronaut of today is the world's most prestigious popular idol. Once launched into space he holds in his hands something far more costly and precious than the millions of dollars' worth of equipment in his capsule; he holds the prestige and the honor of his country." An earlier *Time* magazine article had exalted this feeling of nationalism that the space program seemed to evoke in everyone and was ecstatic when describing a very rare week in the early, accident-prone U.S. space program when two back-to-back successes were recorded. A gas-filled balloon and a satellite had both been sent into space without mishap, and the torrent of words almost danced off the page: "At a time when political charge and countercharge revved the air waves, when a kind of national self-examination was going on, and when reports of declining U.S. prestige abroad could be politically magnified into charges that the United States had become a second-class power, a dazzling succession of achievement did much to restore U.S. pride last week. The space program was perceived as containing the entire country's psyche, mind, subconscious, spirit, and patriotism within its successes and failures." The President's Special Assistant for Science and Technology, feeling the tug of the competition and nationalism, put it this way: "During the next few years the prestige of the United States will in part be determined by the leadership we demonstrate in space activities."

Each woman candidate seemed to intuitively grasp the depth of the privilege which might be bestowed on her and reflected it in her reverential approach to its possibility. But transcending this thought was one even more pressing: eventually everything came down to only one point. Time and again each candidate displayed a readiness to begin the journey immediately, and they all wanted to know only one thing—"When do we start?"

In an ironic stroke of timing, on February 20, 1962 (the day that John Glenn went into space), NASA Administrator James Webb, the same man who had asked Jerrie to become a consultant, issued a memo to all NASA employees. It stated, "It is my intention to take positive steps to ensure equal opportunity for employment and advancement for all qualified persons on the sole basis of merit and fitness without discrimination on the basis of sex. I expect NASA employees at all organizational levels to give full support and cooperation to this program." It took many years, however, for that policy to take hold at the deepest levels of NASA's manned space organization.

Today, federal policy has been written to encourage, by statute, the inclusion of a diverse work population in all federal organizations, including the NASA astronaut corps. This was an immense boost for the women who wanted to become astronauts during the 1970s and 1980s and the policy should for all practical purposes make gender a moot point in astronaut selection. Additionally, the NASA organizational value statement, as shown in its recent strategic plan, emphasizes the need to "build a team of highly qualified individuals that is representative, at all levels, of America's diversity."

Chapter Eleven

In retrospect, considering the massive effort it has taken for women to achieve the levels of equality they enjoy today, for the Mercury Thirteen to have been allowed into the space program in 1960 would have been a miracle. Copious layers of rationalization were used to deny them this honor. The most insidious (but never discussed) argument against them being allowed into the ranks of astronauts—and maybe the most compelling argument, the one that is implied over and over again when trying to understand the futility of their efforts—was that their very presence threatened NASA and the entire space program. The premise used by NASA and other federal proponents to ensure that the programs would be funded in the huge amounts required was that space travel was dangerous, glamorous, and sexy. In one adoring news article written soon after the Mercury Seven were chosen, they were described as "bronzed, lean, healthy, [and] keen-eyed."

This was the era of manly, heroic action movies with John Wayne, and real life had to reflect the fiction within which the country was living. If NASA had allowed women to become part of the program, it would have done two things: it would have made space travel seem easy because "even women can do it," and it would have taken the men's hero status away, especially that of the Mercury Seven. They seemed to be special to everyone; even the astronauts who entered the space program subsequent to the initial group treated them as though they were something other than men. The Mercury Seven were considered the most manly of men; without the macho overtones, the American public, and consequently Congress, might not have been so enamored with the entire process and might have abandoned it.

Whether the original Lovelace tests were done on the thirteen women as a medical control group or whether they were actually being considered as the first class of women to be qualified as astronauts is hard to prove, but this author believes that they were potential candidates until NASA decided that the moment at hand was not the right time for it to associate itself with women. Dr. Don Kilgore recently made an insightful comment when he pointed to a striking difference among some of the attitudes; he said that "NASA was not ready for women," not that the country was not ready for them.

At least one test, the sensory isolation test in Oklahoma City, was more difficult for the women than for the Mercury Seven. The women had passed it by setting endurance records. At the NASA Conference on the Peaceful Uses of Space in Tulsa, Oklahoma, Dr. Lovelace spoke openly of the women's testing regimen being essentially "the same detailed and comprehensive physical examinations, laboratory tests, X-ray examinations, and physical competence tests as the male astronauts had." Dr. Don Kilgore of the Lovelace Clinic recently confirmed that the testing regimen was exactly the same as that given to the Mercury Seven and that in some areas the women had tested better than some of the astronauts.

Dr. Shurley, who was the principal investigator during the Veterans Administration Hospital psychological testing of phase II, titled all his findings from Jerrie Cobb's testing with the notation "woman astronaut," as did Dr. Lovelace in phase I. All the articles written about the women's program during August 1960 after Dr. Lovelace's announcement of its existence were proof positive that the United States was about to launch a woman astronaut. In addition, despite protestations that NASA had never thought or planned for the inclusion of women astronauts, Brigadier General Don Flickinger of the Air Force's School

of Aviation Medicine and consultant to NASA on all matters pertain-
ing to the Mercury Seven qualifications, had considered and listed the
basic requirements of women astronauts as early as September 1961.
They included the requirement that the women be flat chested, have
a pilot's license, be under thirty-five years of age, and (contrary to
what Jackie Cochran had thought) be married. This, of course, begs
the question of disqualification because of too much of a good thing.
If a well-endowed woman pilot qualified to become an astronaut in
all areas except those of measurements, could she be disqualified
based on her breast size?

Another issue that created uncertainty as to the women's status was
the fact that they all maintained the secrecy that had been requested
of them until late in the program. It most certainly worked against
them and sheltered NASA from having to make a commitment. By
keeping quiet, the issue was never pressed with NASA as to whether
they were, in fact, astronaut trainees. By making the program public
knowledge from the beginning, the women could have at least forced
the issue with NASA and the military training centers so that their
work and emotional energy would not have been expended if there
had been disavowal at the outset. Secrecy allowed the program to
continue with no oversight, no credibility, and no commitment on the
part of the space program with no advantage for the women but with
every advantage for the space agency. If at some point it had become
politically imperative that it provide a "first" which the United States
so desperately needed, NASA could have, with minimal training,
launched any number of these women on practically a moment's
notice. But since it never became critical, they never had to acknowledge the women's existence.

There were others who evidently thought the women were about
to become astronauts. Dr. Lovelace's letter to each potential woman
candidate clearly stated that it was an invitation to be considered for

the Women in Space program, and went further to mention the requirements for women astronauts. Equally as telling, during the Congressional hearings before the Special Subcommittee on the Selection of Astronauts in July 1962, Representative Anfuso repeatedly referred to the thirteen women as astronauts.

There also has been considerable significance attached to the argument that NASA did not even know about the tests; this has to be wishful thinking by the detractors of the Mercury Thirteen. According to Jerrie Cobb's book, *Woman into Space*, her introduction in September 1959 to the entire concept was made by two men, Dr. Lovelace and General Donald Flickinger. Despite the fact that he was in the U.S. Air Force, by this time General Flickinger was deeply involved in the space program at NASA and the Mercury program and had been instrumental in determining the original qualifications for the Mercury Seven. He was very much aware of the testing protocol that Dr. Lovelace had designed and to which he was subjecting the women throughout the entire duration of the program.

Another overwhelming obstacle, impossible to overcome was the lack of support from one of their own. Even though Jacqueline Cochran was past the age of hoping to become an astronaut, she could have probably bullied a program into existence. It would have been for the glory of people other than herself, however, and she was not good at that. She declared to Jerrie Cobb that she would have liked to have been the first woman in space, "but after nearly thirty years of flying I decided that I could serve the others best by not becoming a competitor with them as an active participant." Despite this proclamation, Cochran must have had a change of heart, for when Janie Hart met with her moments prior to the Congressional hearings, she later said that it was clear the Jackie was not going to be a supporter of the thirteen women. In fact, Hart said that Jackie Cochran "shafted" the women during the hearings and she speculated that it was because Jackie had recently sustained a permanent injury that disqualified her from ever going into space and she couldn't face having someone else go instead.

There is also a noticeable discrepancy in the documentation that concerned the level of participation by Jacqueline Cochran in choosing and funding the initial group of pilots and testing. In the entire book *Woman into Space* by Jerrie Cobb and Jane Rieker, in which Jerrie describes the initial contact and subsequent choosing of the pilots to be tested, Jackie Cochran's contribution is never mentioned. Yet when Cochran was asked to testify before Congress about the subject, she took all the credit for determining the names of the pilots to be tested and even discussed the amount of money she provided to ensure that all the women were able to travel to Albuquerque. According to another of the Mercury Thirteen, Cochran had not been invited to participate at all in the initial determination of candidates, and when she found out that something was afoot at the Lovelace Clinic, she gave her "good friend" Randy Lovelace a piece of her mind until she was let in. In fairness, Dr. Lovelace's associates at the clinic remember Jackie as being involved almost from the beginning. Either way, she had a reputation of having her way and getting credit for it. She also had a way of making lifelong enemies through some of her tactics.

During the 1940s, when Cochran was developing and selling her idea of a women's auxiliary flying force to the military, she had competition from a woman named Nancy Love. Love founded an organization called the Women's Auxiliary Ferry Squadron (WAFS), which was ultimately merged into Cochran's organization; Cochran became the director of the entire women's flying effort during World War II, and Love was the commander of nothing. She may have had that same sort of idea for the Women in Space program as well. No matter her motives, without Jackie's help and with a mountain of criticism coming from all over the nation, the women had very little chance of persuading NASA to take a chance.

A *New York Times* interview with Mrs. James A. Lovell and Mrs. James A. McDivitt personified the feelings of a lot of the nation; both astronaut wives showed the level of dissent when they gave the following quotes. Mrs. Lovell said, "I don't think they ever found a woman capable of being an astronaut. I think they would have a lot of problems on a long journey if they took a woman along." Mrs. McDivitt added, "They sure would. I would hope the space program would be smart enough not to take them into the program. And that's not because I don't want one going on a flight with my husband." In fact, no one in the nation was willing to have a woman fly with her husband.

In summary documentation provided to the Subcommittee on the Selection of Astronauts, Cochran basically disavowed any notion that the thirteen women were being tested with the thought of their becoming astronauts. She also maintained (wrongly, it turns out) that the battery of medical tests that all thirteen women completed at the Lovelace Clinic were not the complete set. Even though the women maintain that they volunteered for the testing, Cochran stated that she had to "dig up" additional candidates when Jerrie was the only one to volunteer. In her summary statement, she took the opportunity to take a swipe at Jerrie and Janie for presuming to represent all the other eleven trainees. In the end, as stated in an article written by Lillian Kozloski and Maura Mackowski in *Final Frontier*, it may have been her own words that explained why she was not a wholehearted supporter of the thirteen women—she was an associate of the soon-to-be president Lyndon Johnson and had plans for herself: "She had a lifetime of achievements in a man's world, they say and when age made it time to gracefully step aside, she just couldn't give a hand up to another women."

Jackie talked of her dreams for her place in space: "I had every intention of following my high-performance aircraft adventures with a

trip into space." Throughout her life, she had learned that almost anything was possible if one had a plan from which one would not be
discouraged. She had learned this lesson as she had pulled herself up
from the depths of poverty to the status of international businesswoman.

She had created plan after plan that she put into motion and successfully executed. First, she decided that if she saved money, she
would be able to buy herself a business. Then she had planned the
expansion of that business with the use of a pilot's license. Next she
had seen a way to international fame through the use of her aviator's
skills. She meticulously planned each endeavor and more often than
not, the plan worked out just as she had foreseen it. There is no reason to believe that she had, at this point in her life, abandoned a
process that had brought her so much success. If she thought there
was a way for her to become the first woman into space, this idea
may have compelled her to be a harsh critic of the thirteen women's
efforts. If she had helped others take that first step as women into
space, it would have most likely ruined any chance that she might
have had, and it would certainly have precluded her from being the
first American woman into space. She was not one to take second
place in any endeavor.

Approximately one year after her testimony before Congress in
June 1962, Jacqueline Cochran was appointed to the consultant's position in NASA that Jerrie had held. Maybe this was the first step in a
well thought out plan for Jackie to become the first woman in space.
Unfortunately, during the time she held the position, NASA came no
closer to a Women in Space program.

Gene Nora Jessen had another take on the outcome of the hearings and the Women in Space program, and why the women were not
allowed to join in on the fun. She said that while Cochran's testimony
created bitterness among the women, ultimately "it was pretty much
a foregone conclusion that the Mercury astronauts had thrown their
weight around and seen to it that there were no women in the pro-

gram." Wally Funk basically agreed that they didn't have a chance. "It was clearly a good-old-boy network at that point." It was made very clear from the beginning that the men didn't want the women in the program and considered them a distraction. To make matters even more difficult, one of the Mercury Seven, Deke Slayton, was named as the head of the Manned Spacecraft Center's Astronaut Selection Board. He was, in fact, made the keeper of the keys of astronaut selection, and no one was allowed to enter into the kingdom of the astronaut corps without his approval. Deke was considered one of the astronauts without poetry; that is, he was a strictly by-the-book kind of person and did not dally with concepts that were so far out of the normal spectrum as women astronauts. He was very forceful, in a subtle way, and when he became negative about an idea, there was no changing his mind. With these kinds of pressures, NASA apparently chose not to approach the issue at all.

This denial of support took place even though there was a culture-defining movement sweeping the country concerning equality for women, including equal employment opportunities. In an effort to at least give lip service to this movement, NASA published an Administrator's Memorandum on Equal Employment. It stated, in part, "Women are entitled to equality of opportunity for employment in Government and in industry. But a mere statement supporting equality of opportunity must be implemented by affirmative steps to see that the doors are really open for training, selection, advancement, and equal pay." This pledge to ensure that women were given equal training and advancement was ignored and downplayed for years to come. Even President Johnson termed the lack of women astronauts as wasting a national resource, but chose to do nothing constructive about it. Considering some of their detractors, it's a wonder that women astronauts were ever allowed into existence at NASA. As late as August 1974, a mere four years before the first women were to become astronauts, the argument regarding whether to allow women into the corps raged on in periodicals such as *Time* magazine. Astronaut Mike Collins ignited a firestorm and noted science fiction author Arthur C. Clark fanned the flames of rebellion during a written exchange discussing how distracting women's breasts might be in space. There were references to "bobbing breasts" and an agreement between the two men that certain well-endowed women should not be allowed to become astronauts based on their physiology.

Late in his career, even George Low admitted that NASA's record for bringing women into meaningful career positions, including that of astronaut, was poor at best. In a letter dated August 14, 1973, Low writes, "I agree with your observation that our record in bringing women into higher level positions in NASA is very poor." It wasn't until the January 1978 class of astronauts that any women were ever qualified to be included. For this to happen, the main disqualifier for the thirteen original women, test pilot experience, had been downgraded to "highly desirable" for pilot astronauts only, and was not even required for other members of the team, the mission, and payload specialists positions.

Another debate raged within NASA for the first several decades of the space program, and women were caught up in its backlash as well. The argument was between the scientific purists, who wanted to explore space with unmanned vehicles, and those who wanted to add humans to the mix. The unmanned missions would have been able to launch heavier payloads on each trip because all the equipment needed to sustain a human would have been unnecessary.

The other side of the conflict held that without on-site human intervention, missions could be lost; besides, without the human element, the public would not have had any interest in space exploration. There would have been a serious diminution of the program's stature and therefore an attendant alteration in the budget could have been expected. If women had been allowed to participate in any of the space launches, the scientific purists would have had enough ammunition to potentially sink the effort. They could have maintained that the manned missions were so unimportant as to involve a woman; therefore, the unmanned missions were more valuable and should take precedence in the budget battle. This would have created a funding crisis; it was not worth the risk of losing the interest of the admiring public by chancing a woman astronaut. All the money used to support the space program came from the taxes of working people, and any change in the allure of the space program might have brought with it a demand that government funds be directed instead to domestic programs for immediate, visible benefit. In other words, if women had been allowed to go into space, the public might not have been enchanted enough to continue to support that kind of financial outlay by the government.

By this time in the space race, Congress and the president had poured hundreds of millions of dollars into the program, with even more scheduled for fiscal years 1963 ($3.7 billion) and 1964 ($6 billion). So it was in NASA's best interest to keep the program dramatic and dangerous. This provided a curtain behind which the wizards of NASA could hide, all the while choreographing the hero worship and the ensuing avalanche of dollars into the manned program. As late as March 1969, virtually on the eve of the moon landing, the argument continued to rage, with at least one congressman threatening to stop the entire process. Congressman Joseph E. Karth, from Minnesota, was incensed to find that NASA management was still playing budget games between the manned and the unmanned programs. On finding that NASA had been dragging its feet in funding an important satellite program in order to ensure that the manned flights would have enough justification for existence, he let loose a volley with a press release, saying "I am going to begin saying loudly about this Congress that we may well not need a manned program. It appears to me that this committee and the taxpayer have been had." According to NASA documents, the U.S. public ultimately provided $392 million dollars for the Mercury program, $1.2 billion for the Gemini program, and $21 billion for the Apollo program—yet not a single dime could be spared for the thirteen women.

Compounding everything else was the fact that NASA was a new agency within the federal government. It was a civilian agency, and its embrace on longevity was tenuous. It had only just recently wrested itself away from the generals of the military; if women had been allowed to become astronauts, this one act might have convinced the world that those civilians in NASA had lost their senses. The space program would have been returned to the military fold where there were "real men" to do the job.

President Kennedy's brand-new Special Assistant for Science and Technology, Jerome Wiesner, had in effect just declared war on NASA in a special report he created. It called for the entire reorganization of all of NASA, and strongly criticized its lack of accomplishment. There was a move afoot to return NASA to the Department of Defense in hopes of a better launch record, and there were other foes, from within and without, with all of whom NASA had to deal. The women were just considered another in a long line of these enemies which had to be fended off.

There was another factor at play that was not recognized as such until much later in the decades succeeding the beginning of the space race. The Mercury Seven had reached the summit of their profession, maybe the most highly rated profession of the decade. The original astronauts had been honored with national adulation that had taken the form of ticker-tape parades, headlines in national newspapers, and pictures on the covers of internationally circulated magazines. They had been given exotic automobiles and large life insurance policies. They didn't want anyone in the space corps who could even remotely overshadow them in the areas of talent or public relations; their egos were absorbing it all. Post-Mercury Seven astronauts told stories about how protective the original seven were about their turf and perks. When the members of class number two arrived at NASA and began training, the Mercury Seven never offered to tell them about the potential bounty, much less smooth the way for them to share; they did not want any competition.

Pete Conrad told of times that he traveled with John Glenn after he had been accepted into NASA as an astronaut. As they entered each airport on a trip to one equipment contractor or another, Glenn would be accosted by large crowds wanting autographs. Many times Conrad would wind up carrying the Mercury Seven astronaut's bags in total anonymity while Glenn soaked up the glory of the crowd, giving autographs to all. The magnitude of the men's competitive egos was something the women were never able to assess, much less compete against. The male fear of showing weakness was upstaged by only one other fear: the fear of being equaled or bested by a woman. To a great extent these men had been schooled in this aspect of our competitive culture more deeply than any other factor. They were not about to be put into a position of being beaten by a woman, especially not in such a public forum.

Whether anyone called them astronauts or not, everything came down to this argument: Could they have done the job and could their presence in space have eased the Cold War losses we were experiencing at the hands of the Russians? To a person, the Mercury Thirteen women maintain today that all they wanted was an even chance to train to become astronauts. Even Deke Slayton, who was grounded for medical reasons by the NASA medical board on March 15, 1962, without ever being able to fly a single Mercury mission, was given a second chance when he was allowed to fly as a crew member of the Apollo-Soyuz Test Project. Despite all of the military and test pilot mystique, it is interesting to note that when the dust settled and an astronaut was chosen to be the first human to set foot on the moon, that person turned out to be a civilian; Neil Armstrong was not a member of the military.

Sadly, a single word of enthusiasm from any one of a number of people could have cleared the way for these exceptional women to have become astronauts. President Kennedy, Vice-President Johnson, Congress, NASA, Scott Carpenter, or America's hero John Glenn could have spoken up for it. Janie Hart has said, "Glenn had an opportunity to do something historical" if he had advocated giving the women a chance as astronauts. Instead, all of them ultimately let the concept die, mostly, it seems, because in John Glenn's words, "It would go against the social order of things." By agreeing that the social order of things (the status quo) was more important than doing what was right, or even in this case what was prudent, all of them may have injured the country. This was an opportunity to be bold and broad-minded. Broadness of mind early in the 1960s might have precluded the violent revolt that was needed to overcome the status quo of sexism and racism a few years later. The national damage and humiliation of the 1968 Democratic National Convention, the race riots, the Tailhook scandal, and thousands of other mind-numbing events might have been avoided that have taken an enormous physical and mental toll on this country. The use of true talent of any gender and color might have made us a nation even greater than we are today, but no one was willing to break with the existing social order.

All in all, the thirteen women were at the wrong place at the wrong time. Professional women were of such rarity in that era as to be immediately suspect; to have thirteen of them ready, willing, and just as able as the men was not something that NASA was willing to accept, much less publicize. Nor was the public ready to accept this new status for women. In the same *McCall's* magazine which publicized the thirteen women as astronaut candidates, another article entitled "Does a Wife Have a Right To Work?" contained the following statement, which probably sums up the prevailing mood of the country at that time. "There are still men who take the traditional view that the wife's place is exclusively in the home. This may be a genuine desire to protect and care for a woman, or it may be that such a husband just doesn't want to face any personal discomfort or inconvenience." If this sentiment best described the era which was being written about and published in mainstream magazines, what chance did the thirteen have in leaping across that immense chasm of reality into a world which most people would have considered fantasy?

It was lamented in the June 1963 article for *Life* magazine that in the final analysis, there was a qualified, able, and ready cadre of women who could have been admirable astronauts in the early 1960s, "but for a variety of reasons, including NASA's outstanding lack of enthusiasm, their Women in Space program [was] never able to get off the ground." One, some, or all of these thirteen women should have been allowed to enter into the astronaut training program. They were driven to succeed not only because of their own personalities, but because this endeavor was of such importance to the country. They would not have allowed themselves to fail. It is said that the astronauts who made it into the space program "knew" that they belonged. The Mercury Thirteen "knew" that they belonged as well. In the final analysis, according to NASA, the Women in Space program never existed.

Chapter Twelve

As the U.S. engineers and managers finally wrangled the space program through its initial period of problems, America overwhelmed the Russians with our exploits. Teams of U.S. men went to the moon and back—several times. We sent exploration vessels to Mars and Jupiter. There was even a move afoot to begin a fifteen-year effort for a manned mission to Mars. While this never came to fruition because of pressure on the space program to produce direct benefits for the millions of people still firmly bound to earth, it was an indicator of how far our technology had come.

Changes began to take place in both the Russian and U.S. programs. The original fear and frustration that accompanied the launch of *Sputnik I* no longer frightened the American people. The Iron Curtain fell along with budgets. The post-Apollo space exploration concept was once again being shaped in response to the manned versus the nonmanned argument, so new programs were designed to support both aspects. The nonmanned missions could be sent to the furthest reaches of space in search of our planetary cousins, and the manned missions would be content to remain within relative reach of the earth.

The programs became more commercial and the exploration of space became less of a race and more of a collaboration. International cooperation was emphasized, with the ultimate goal of determining practical applications for the discoveries in space. A call went forth for a space vehicle that was reusable and economical, one that could carry entire crews of astronauts into space on a single trip. The answer was the space shuttle, which became the preferred manned vehicle for U.S. space transportation.

The shuttle is a winged space plane that returns to earth after each mission; it carries into space experiments that have potential impact on the world's population. Its beauty is that it can carry pilots and scientists simultaneously, negating the age-old argument that a vehicle can only carry either astronauts or scientists. It has become the eighteen-wheeler of outer space.

NASA evolved during this time period as well. The nation had just completed a bruising and tumultuous decade during which awareness had swept the nation, awakening women to their potential. Sometime in the early to mid-1970s, NASA and the federal government suddenly realized that nearly half the voting public was female. NASA faced the harsh reality that women had begun to spread their wings and vote their interests independently. As the voting public went, so did the budget. The confluence of the need for nonpiloting scientists to support commercial and social advancements in space, and the availability of so many highly credentialed and talented women, finally crashed through any last barrier NASA could erect and gave women the chance they had been waiting for since 1960.

The ultimate public grace with which NASA embraced women into the space program belied the scramble in the background that they had been going through to bring diversity into its ranks. By 1976, a full-fledged media and outreach campaign had been designed and implemented to reach specialized minority populations. Millions of dollars were spent to entice the type of women (high energy and capable) that only a few years before had been shut out. Letters and specially designed brochures blanketed universities with science and engineering departments that enrolled women students. It became mandatory that a section of all NASA recruiting conferences and symposiums be targeted to women. Evidently, either women were not interested or none believed that they would be seriously considered by NASA, because the response in 1976 was so tepid as to be thought nonexistent.

The communiqués flying around NASA were typically low key in their language, but the fact that they existed at all indicated that matters were becoming serious. One letter noted that the problem was not improving: "It has been six months since NASA issued a call for Space Shuttle Astronaut Candidates. As of this date [November 23, 1976] the response from minority and female candidates has been less than satisfactory." The directive continued with the instruction that females and minorities be made the number one recruitment target until conditions changed. It closed by stating "We must do more." The NASA recruiting team redoubled its efforts and had more special brochures developed, which were sent to the heads of science and engineering departments at selected schools. A concerted effort was made to contact women's scientific organizations to ask for assistance in recruiting. The efforts paid off, for the response to the call for astronauts for 1978 brought an avalanche of applications. NASA must have heaved a sigh of relief when 1,544 of the applications proved to be from women; not just any women, but women of such talent, education, and intelligence as to make one wonder what damage the nation had sustained by excluding them for so long.

There have been forty-three women chosen to be astronauts during the last twenty-plus years. From the class of 1978 until the class of 2000, the women's credentials have included degrees too numerous to count in subjects as varied as aerospace engineering, medicine, geophysics, environmental engineering, and phycology. (Table 1 in the appendix provides a complete list of the modern women astronauts and their academic credentials.) Several of these women are graduates of the U.S. military academies. Some of them are veterans of U.S. military actions in Grenada and Desert Storm. Many have thousands of hours of flying time; some were test pilots at the two military test pilot schools. They participate in a vast array of extracurricular activities, and several of them are wives and mothers. All in all, they have a surprising number of characteristics in common with the Mercury Thirteen including their willingness to make sacrifices in order to become astronauts.

Sally Ride in a 1978 NASA crew photo. (courtesy NASA)

Chapter Thirteen

In 1978, the first six women chosen to train to become astronauts were Shannon Lucid, Sally Ride, Judith Resnik, Margaret Rhea Seddon, Kathryn Sullivan, and Anna Fisher. The six had much in common, but many differences as well. As their parts in history unfolded, it was the talent that each of them brought to NASA that became the most important aspect of their participation, not the fact that they were women—but it took quite a while for everyone to realize that.

Jerrie Cobb stood outside the Kennedy Space Center fence and watched the launch that took Sally Ride into space, once again reveling in someone else's victory, but wondering if hers would ever come. Janie Hart watched that day too, with the same disappointment that Jerrie was feeling. Unfortunately, this would not be the last time they were to stand outside that fence and watch a launch carry another lucky person into space on a ride that they might have taken themselves.

Sally Ride hadn't envisioned a life as a heroine, but in her own mind had simply grown up thinking that she could be anything or do anything she wanted. She became an early tennis star, with talent enough to catch the eye of tennis great Billie Jean King. A good student in high school, she ultimately graduated from Stanford with a bachelor's degree in physics which she used to narrow her field of interest into X-ray astronomy and free electron laser research. As she neared the completion of her doctorate at Stanford, an article in the Stanford student newspaper discussing the need for scientists at NASA to become specialists on board the shuttle caught her eye. This article was, apparently, the result of NASA's redoubled recruitment efforts in 1976. She decided to apply, and her application became one of the 8,079 applications NASA received from people all over the United States vying to become members of NASA's astronaut class of 1978. After a long wait, Sally was finally determined to be one of the six successful women astronaut candidates.

At the time, Ride said she was sure that despite a historical perspective implying otherwise, some of the women were sure to be selected this time. "Women in space were inevitable. At the very least they need us up there for biological experiments." NASA accepted the six women astronauts with a newly found enthusiasm. A public information officer explained the changed attitude by saying, "Maybe the whole space program has matured enough so that we can now settle down to the business of space flight." NASA historian Glen Swanson maintained that two factors contributed to the first women being brought into the mix. He said that there were fewer unknowns, which was another interpretation of what had been stated twenty years earlier, when the men testifying before Congress said that women would be welcome when space travel became safe. As for the second factor, Swanson agreed that it would have been political folly to have continued to ground women, because the women's movement had become a force to be reckoned with even by NASA. The world was returning to "normal" with the scars of the Vietnam War beginning to heal after the 1973 pullout of Vietnam and Nixon resigning the presidency after the Watergate scandal; the nation needed something else to which to turn its attention. Whatever the reason, these women were welcomed and mostly allowed to get on with their business.

By this time, the nation had been through drastic cultural changes in the way it considered women and women's potential. The National Organization for Women had burst on the scene as an outgrowth of the movement personified in Betty Friedan's book *The Feminine*

Mystique written in 1963. A constitutional amendment guaranteeing all women equal rights was circulating among the states for ratification, and women were being allowed into the military academies.

All six of the women astronauts were media shy, but Judith Resnik seemed more so than the others. She was a quiet, private person by nature so when she was chosen as one of NASA's first women astronauts, she was more than distressed by the glare of attention trained on the women. The interest was manifested in many ways, most of them trite. After selection, while the entire class of new astronauts was training at the Water Survival Training program near Homestead Air Force Base, the press hounded the women and once again turned to things familiar. In their daily press filings with their respective news outlets, the reporters took note of the number of the six women who had bothered to wear makeup (none) and the number who were wearing jewelry (one). One paper wrote, "Seddon was the only one wearing jewelry doing the exercises—gold studs in her petite ears." It was also noted that there were five brunettes and a blond. Resnik displayed her annoyance when asked about the significance of being a woman in the astronaut corps, and tried to explain. "We're all astronauts. We'll be going through the same training as the men. We'll have the same problems thrown at us, and we'll have to solve them in the same ways. There are no benefits or hardships in being a woman." Less than eight years later she would have again been distressed at the glare of the spotlight on her as the first woman astronaut to die in the line of duty when the *Challenger* exploded seventy-eight seconds after launch.

Resnik had begun her career in the engineering field in 1970, subsequent to graduation from Carnegie-Mellon University with an electrical engineering degree. A few years later, she earned a doctorate from the University of Maryland and worked for the likes of RCA and Xerox. After assessing NASA as the place that would give her the career of her dreams, she decided to apply to become an astronaut; she had heard NASA was looking to add women to the 1978 roster of candidates. To even her odds, she began a serious physical conditioning program and also added flying lessons to her schedule.

As an astronaut, she finally got to see in action the remote manipulation system that she and Sally Ride helped design and create as part of their collateral duties at NASA. Her first flight into space was also the new space shuttle *Discovery's* maiden voyage. Pictures of her on the mission were captured, with her long, curly hair floating weightless, highlighted against the shuttle work areas in the background.

With the unusual middle name of Rhea, Margaret Rhea Seddon had more in common with the original women of the Mercury Thirteen than just the name she shared with Rhea Allison Woltman. She wanted to be an astronaut, but was afraid that NASA might not be ready when she was. She was a pilot just like the Mercury Thirteen, and she had become a member of "The 99's," the international women pilots' association, just like they had. She was also a very skilled surgeon with a medical degree from the University of Tennessee College of Medicine. Unknown to most, she had long harbored an ambition other than medicine; when asked after being chosen about her impetus for becoming an astronaut she said, "I'd always thought being an astronaut would be a neat thing to do. I didn't know if the space program would ever be open to women."

Her timing could not have been any better. Her field of specialization after being accepted to the astronaut corps also set her apart. She wanted to study the effects of space travel on the female metabolism and to disprove that "women's monthly hormonal cycles make them unfit to be astronauts and presidents." Aspiring to put to scientific rest the argument women had waged since trying to fly every day of the month beginning with the WASPs, she too was often distressed with the pronounced emphasis the press placed on things of no significance. But all in all, she seemed able to keep a sense of humor about most of it. During training at Homestead Air Force Base, the photographers had been relentless. At one point, as she was preparing to execute part of a training exercise a photographer shouted, "Hold it, miss." She good-naturedly shouted back a reminder, "It's doctor."

In the mid-1950s Shannon Lucid (then in the eighth grade) wrote a research paper discussing the subject of rocket research, arguing, "If the science shortage is in such dire status as they claim, they'd let women in on the same ground as men." This perceptive observation was made by a teenager a full four years before Jerrie Cobb and Dr. Lovelace held their first meeting on the beach in Miami to discuss women becoming astronaut trainees. This intuitive young woman continued to harbor a secret interest in space exploration for many years while she made stops for a husband, several college degrees, and three children. She finally got her wish when she made it into the astronaut class of 1978.

She accumulated several thousand hours of flying time and had designs on becoming a pilot for a commercial airline before she heard about NASA's call for astronauts. Out of the over 8,000 applications it received in response to the outreach of 1978, her application was reportedly the first one to reach NASA.

Lucid was impatient with outsiders and the press when asked to explain how she managed to be an astronaut and a mother too. She told them, "We do the same work as the men, yet nobody asks them about how their kids feel about their work." When chosen at the age of thirty-five, she was the oldest woman to become an astronaut; when she flew into space on June 17, 1985, on her first mission aboard the shuttle *Discovery* she was forty-two years old, almost exactly the same age as Janie Hart when she testified before Congress in 1962. With five missions under her belt, Lucid currently holds the record for being in space longer than any other U.S. astronaut, male or female: 223 days.

Despite her longtime experience in space, her credentials were questioned prior to her last and most historic mission on board the Russian space station *Mir.* Even before she arrived, her Russian hosts

With her historic six-month stay aboard the *Mir* completed, Shannon Lucid accepts a congratulatory phone call from President Bill Clinton. (courtesy NASA)

had told the press that they could hardly wait for her arrival because "we know that women love to clean." The Russian cosmonauts had apparently not heard about the equalization of the genders and were reading from a 1962 script. Despite all the initial advances their program had made by launching women into space, somehow they had begun to take on attitudes similar to the U.S. program of an earlier time.

Even with this inauspicious beginning, the mission was a raging success. Shannon was responsible for numerous scientific experiments, including a significant one on her own body. She was relentless about her physical conditioning and worked out each day so that even after six months of weightlessness, she surprised everyone by walking unaided off the space shuttle after it landed. When Lucid returned home, she was awarded the Congressional Space Medal of Honor, only the ninth of its kind ever to be awarded and the first ever bestowed on a woman. (John Glenn is a fellow recipient.) In an equally exciting tribute, the Order of Friendship was given to her by President Boris Yeltsin of Russia.

Another of the six was Kathryn Sullivan. Her first love in the realm of education was geology, and the thought of seeing the configuration of the earth from space was a source of immense inspiration for her. Sullivan was twenty-six years old when chosen by NASA in 1978 to join the program. Her love of things terrestrial was the key to her pursuit of a place in space. She said, "The idea of being able to look back at the earth from orbit is truly exciting to me." Ironically, it was the other way around for many of her fellow astronauts, who had to go into space before they had discovered the earth.

On *Apollo 8*, during the first mission to orbit the moon, astronaut Bill Anders reached the profound realization that while he and the crew had flown thousands of miles to orbit the moon, they had actually, through photographs and film, discovered the earth in all of its fragility. The "earth rise" photograph taken on this mission, showing the brilliantly colored blue-and-white earth just as it peeked above the moon's rim, is one of the most important photographs of all time. It served to emphasize what Sullivan and others wanted, which was to protect the huge, delicate planet on which all humans depend for life. Sullivan's first flight occurred in October 1984, aboard the shuttle *Challenger* where, to her amazement, she became the first U.S. woman to walk in space. She stepped outside to prove that routine mission support work could be done by individuals outside the protection of a spacecraft. She was as mystified as the other five women astronauts at the press's response to her and the other members of the class of 1978; even the most minute details of each of their lives were reported. She said, "the thing I find hard to swallow is the fascination with such inane things, like how many times I've played racquetball in a week." Kathryn earned a doctorate in geophysics from Dalhousie University (located in Halifax, Nova Scotia) and developed a specialty in marine geology before applying to NASA.

Many of these women, as well as others, had long aspired to be astronauts. They had been excited by the Mercury Seven and like Anna Fisher, from the class of 1978, they had their first crush on astronaut Alan Shepard, the first American launched into space. Fisher decided she wanted to be an astronaut, but like a lot of the other women, she never let it be known: "It was such a preposterous thought that I could do something like that myself, and I knew people would laugh, so I didn't talk about it." Continuing to quietly harbor this aspiration, she decided that becoming a medical doctor would most likely give her the best shot at being noticed by NASA's selection board. She started with a degree in chemistry from UCLA and later added a medical degree. It was the exact credential for which the board was looking. She rode her first shuttle into space on November 8, 1984, and became the first mother to fly in space. Coincidentally, her husband, Bill, became an astronaut three years later in the class of 1981, giving new impetus to the editorial speculation that began twenty-five years earlier that husband-and-wife teams would fly into space together.

During the previous twenty years, the press had become used to painting a picture of the male astronauts in the program as being identical: strong jawed and fearless. Quite predictably, the same press community tried to portray these six women as cookie-cutter replicas of each other as well. This could not have been further from the truth. Resnik tried to make the point many times that the women were not unique among the astronaut corps. When discussing the classes of 1978 and 1980, she wanted everyone to understand: "We are eight individuals who approach things eight different ways. All that counts is being efficient in what you do." As usual, though, the press continued to focus on the things most comfortable to them and their readership.

As a member of the class of 1980, Mary Cleave was another ambitious, superachieving young woman who was, like Kathryn Sullivan, worried about the damage being done to the earth. She wanted to go into space to ensure that humans didn't do the same thing there. Cleave's consuming passion from the age of ten was model airplanes, and within the following few years those airplanes became real as she earned her pilot's license. She, like Mercury Thirteen member Bernice Steadmen, earned her pilot's license even before she earned her driving license. With a degree from Colorado State University in biology and after a stint teaching, she returned to school at Utah State University, where she earned another degree in phycology. She continued there and finally emerged with a doctorate in both civil and environmental engineering. So armed, she became a sanitary engineer for the Utah Water Research Laboratory, where she first met up with the good-old-boy network. As she went about her work each day, her colleagues at the laboratory discouraged her, saying, "this job is not for women," but Mary refused to allow her coworkers' attitudes to disturb her. Instead, she went about her business of becoming good enough to earn a place on NASA's team. She missed making the class of 1978, but was accepted into the class of 1980. In retrospect, because of NASA's reputation, it astonished Mary, as it had Anna

Fisher from the previous class, that she had found more problems in achieving equality in her chosen profession than she did in NASA. Anna noted later that being a female doctor had its problems: "As an emergency medicine specialist, I found more resistance to women from older doctors than from older astronauts." Considering their experiences, the original thirteen women would have been amazed to hear this.

Bonnie Dunbar's (class of 1980) master's thesis from the University of Washington was done on the field of mechanisms and kinetics of ionic diffusion in sodium beta-alumina. While at the university, she actually participated in research done for the thermal tiles that would keep the space shuttle *Columbia* safe from the searing heat which develops on reentering the earth's atmosphere. Even though she fell in love with the ship she was working on, like others before her, she was reticent to discuss the possibility of becoming a member of a shuttle crew: "When you go to school and pick out a major, you don't say 'I'm going to be an astronaut.'" Cut in the final round of the class of 1978, after reviewing the resumés of the successful six women who had made the grade Dunbar decided she should round out her interests. She went to work in the NASA complex of Johnson Space Center as a systems engineer, and in 1980 from 2,880 applicants was chosen as a member of that class.

Five additional women astronauts were selected in the classes of 1984 and 1985. They were bright and enthusiastic about their first opportunity to fly on the shuttle. But by this time, the process had become so routine that there was no press to be seen until October 5, 1984, when Kathryn Sullivan and Sally Ride were launched together as part of the shuttle crew aboard the *Challenger* in what was to be two firsts for the United States. When this mission was announced, it was saluted as the one on which a woman would go into space for a second time, and also the mission during which the first trip outside an orbiting spaceship would be accomplished by a woman. These firsts excited the press out of their stupor and instigated a frenzy of coverage, exciting the world. The coverage seemed to put the Russians on the defensive again; in a classic move reminiscent of the Cold War 1960s, the Russians, without much notice, launched *Soyuz T-12* on July 17, 1984, two and a half months before the U.S. shuttle launch, with a woman, Svetlana Savitskaya, on board. During the trip, she left the spaceship on a task called an extravehicular activity (EVA), becoming the first woman in the world to do so. She had effectively trumped NASA's bid to have Sullivan become the first woman to accomplish an EVA, and since the same voyage was Svetlana's second ride into space this also trumped Sally Ride's second-voyage headlines.

Chapter Fourteen

Suddenly, the unthinkable happened. On a cold January day in 1986, only seconds after launch, the shuttle *Challenger* exploded, killing everyone aboard, including one of the original women astronauts chosen in 1978, Judith Resnik, who was intelligent, talented, and well liked. Christa McAuliffe, the first teacher to journey into space, was also lost. This accident brought the manned space exploration missions to a screeching halt. When the cause of the accident was finally determined to have been a weak joint-sealing ring on one of the rocket boosters, months of study and reengineering took place before additional flights were scheduled. The dearth of flights also signaled a decline in astronaut recruitment, but only temporarily. By June 1987, the next class of astronauts was chosen. Mae Jemison and Jan Davis were aware of the newly highlighted dangers, but just like their Mercury Thirteen predecessors, felt that even in the face of danger, the chance to become astronauts was too great to give up. So the shuttle missions continued.

Jemison had received her chemical engineering degree in 1977 from Stanford University. She went on to earn her medical degree from Cornell University and eventually joined the Peace Corps, which assigned her to West Africa. On her return to the United States, she became a general practitioner in California, at the same time pursuing her other interest of engineering. When Jemison was selected to become an astronaut, she made history as the first African American female to be chosen as a member of the team.

Her classmate, Jan Davis, earned several degrees, including a bachelor's in biology from the Georgia Institute of Technology, a bachelor's in mechanical engineering from Auburn University, and a master's and doctorate in mechanical engineering from the University of Alabama at Huntsville. Growing up in Huntsville, Alabama, she went to school with the children of the famed German scientist and father of the American space program, Dr. Wernher von Braun. She remembers the constant image of von Braun and of being inspired by the presence of this great scientist in her hometown. She put her education to work first for Texaco, and then at NASA, where prior to becoming an astronaut, she worked on projects such as the Hubble Telescope and the redesign of the shuttle solid rocket booster external tank attachment ring. She considers becoming an astronaut as the fulfillment of a dream.

Despite bringing these women onboard to become astronauts and working very hard to allay public concerns that NASA was an all-white, male bastion, in selecting the class of 1987 NASA became embroiled in yet another recruitment fiasco reminiscent of the exclusivity found by the Mercury Thirteen women. Accusations and counteraccusations boiled into public view at about the same time that the class of 1987 members were announced. Despite the fact that this class included the first African American female, the press and members of Congress declared it too limited in its outlook to have been fair. Even though by this time NASA had gotten pretty good at recruiting enough women and minorities to make most of its constituencies happy, it had gotten into the habit of hiring almost exclusively from the military test pilot ranks for the shuttle commander and pilot's positions, and from its own technical ranks for the mission specialist positions. This gave the impression that only test pilots had a chance to become shuttle pilots, and was in direct contradiction to NASA's own policy that dictated a fair, national selection method.

The *New York Times* highlighted this process in one of several articles written during this time, dashing the everyday American's dreams of becoming an astronaut by saying, "The idea that any qualified American could become an astronaut has given way to the reality that almost no one outside the military services or the space agency has a chance." The article went on to describe the efforts NASA goes through each year to encourage civilians from outside the agency to apply. Statistics revealed that civilians had a slim chance of being chosen, with the conclusion that all applicants that did not work for NASA or the military were virtually excluded. As noted in various newspapers in the summer of 1987, "Of the forty-five candidates chosen to enter astronaut training since 1984, only two were not employed by the military services or NASA."

In a twist that would have interested some of the original thirteen women, it turned out that one of the two "outsiders" who emerged as successful candidates turned out to be David Low, the son of their former nemesis, George Low, who had testified at the 1962 hearings against the Mercury Thirteen. Even as recently as the class of 1998, NASA's tendency toward organizational nepotism showed no signs of abating. Out of the twenty-five astronauts selected in 1998, eight were members of the Johnson Space Center workforce. Several others were associated with pseudo–NASA organizations such as the Jet Propulsion Laboratory in Pasadena, California.

There was concern that this process was going to alienate most of the needed talent pool, but a greater problem was the possibility of alienating the public after the space program's hiatus as a result of the *Challenger* accident. Confidence in the infallibility of American technology had been a victim of the disaster and had resulted in the sudden public debate whether American lives were worth the risk of this very unreliable technology. The United States was collecting itself after the *Challenger* accident and wanted to put everything back the way it was. NASA was struggling with public perception that the status quo was what the American people wanted; they didn't want to go against it any more now than they had twenty-five years earlier. Returning to a previous time, of course, was not possible, but by pursuing things familiar, the hurt and shock of losing members of the NASA community was lessened.

There was another part of the status quo that NASA didn't want to challenge either. There was a difference between these first women whom NASA had chosen to become astronauts and the original thirteen: all of the women chosen up to this point for work on the shuttle were mission specialists; that is, they were chosen for their technical qualifications and capabilities for completing technical, engineering, and scientific tasks during orbit, not to fly the ship. The Mercury Thirteen women were all pilots and wanted to continue to be so in space. So, despite the importance of having women in the astronaut corps, the barrier that Jerrie Cobb, Janie Hart, and the eleven others had striven to break, that of flying a spaceship, was still firmly in place. Despite the air of success surrounding Sally Ride as she rode into space in 1983, it could be argued that, as of that date, NASA had still not fulfilled the original dream of the Mercury Thirteen. America still had not equaled the feat of the Russian, Valentina, who had been the pilot of her own spaceship.

(top) Crew of space shuttle mission STS-63: (top left to right) Bernard Harris, Jr., and Michael Foale; (lower left to right) Janice Voss, Eileen Collins (pilot), James Wetherbee (commander), and Vladimir Titov. (courtesy NASA). (bottom) Wally Funk and Eileen Collins at The 99s headquarters in 1994. (courtesy Wally Funk)

Chapter 15

Thrilled though she was when Sally Ride went into space in 1983, Mercury Thirteen member Jerri Truhill said she didn't believe she would live long enough to see the next major barrier broken: a woman shuttle pilot or better yet, a woman shuttle commander. There are two pilot positions on each shuttle crew. The pilot position flies in the right seat and is effectively the copilot. The shuttle commander is the captain of the flight and the mission. Jerri Truhill was wrong on both counts.

The class of 1990 astronauts was chosen and it included five women, but with a couple of differences. Two of the women selected were members of the military, and one of them was to pilot the shuttle. The five were Susan Helms, Janice Voss, Nancy Jane Sherlock, Ellen Ochoa, and Eileen Collins (as the pilot).

Also notable was that despite the efforts of Jacqueline Cochran during the 1962 Congressional hearings as well as others after her, the military academies were finally opened to women; Susan Helms was one of the first to graduate from the Air Force Academy. Just for good measure, she later went to Edwards Air Force Base for test pilot training where she received distinguished graduate honors.

On February 3, 1995, Major Eileen Collins blasted into space aboard *STS-63* as the first woman to hold the position of pilot of an American spacecraft. Collins recognized that she had many people to thank for breaking the early barriers, including the Mercury Thirteen.

(top) Mercury Thirteen at Smithsonian Air and Space Museum in 1995 during taping of NBC television show *Dateline*. (courtesy Michael Althaus)   (bottom) Mercury Thirteen readying for taping of *Dateline* (left to right) Sarah Ratley, Rhea Woltman, Wally Funk, B Steadman, Jerrie Cobb, Janie Hart, Gene Nora Jessen, Jerri Truhill, and K Cagle. (courtesy Michael Althaus)

As a salute to the women who had sacrificed so much before her, she completed the circle by acknowledging the efforts of the thirteen women three decades before her. She sent invitations to the eleven surviving women, asking them to come to the launch of the ground-breaking flight which would carry Collins into space, piloting the shuttle *Discovery*. All the women were very surprised, considering their last experiences with the space program, at the warmth of the welcome from NASA officials when they journeyed to Cape Kennedy. Escorted on a tour of the Kennedy Space Center, they were introduced and honored in the presence of a large crowd of dignitaries. On the first day of the event, they were taken by bus to tour some of the outlying facilities. Chatting quietly among themselves, one was heard to ask if the mission commander would allow pilot Eileen Collins to land the shuttle when it returned to earth a few days later. The male tour guide straightened himself to his full height and let the women know that a mission commander would "never!" allow a woman to land the shuttle. The next day, after the tour guide was informed who had been in his care, he was replaced by a woman.

Despite the first tour guide's attitude, the women were amazed that NASA actually was acknowledging them as having played a part in its history, much less allowing them to share a day of it with Eileen Collins after all these years. Each woman was asked by Collins if there was some special, small item Collins could carry into space for her. Jerrie Cobb gave her a small gold pin shaped like an extinct Indian condor, a symbolic gesture recalling the name people in South America gave to her airplane of hope.

K Cagle later related one of her most thrilling moments during her visit to Collins's 1995 liftoff. She had the opportunity to meet Eileen's entire family during one of the social functions prior to the launch. Collins's grandfather made a point of telling K about his appreciation for what the Mercury Thirteen had done. She recounted the story in the *Macon Telegraph*. "He struggled to his feet and shook my hand,"

Cagle said. "He said 'thank you for paving the way for my grand-daughter.'" K and the others were overcome with pride at that moment, knowing they had helped open a critical door for such a talented woman as Eileen Collins. This acknowledgment has come hard and late for some. Mercury Thirteen member Jerri Truhill still believes that if it had been left up to NASA, they would never have been acknowledged, much less invited: "They failed to acknowledge us until they had to. It's just an embarrassing chapter for them." Truhill also confessed that the emotion of the day mixed in with the emotion of all those many years ago and that during the liftoff, all any of the women could do was stand there and cry. They all believe, "We gave Eileen a past and she gave us a future."

Collins earned two master's degrees in subjects ranging from operations research to space systems management. She grew up on the likes of television programs such as *Star Trek* and *Lost in Space*. She read about the WASPs and Amelia Earhart and yearned to become just like them as she progressed directly from college into Air Force pilot training. She became a flight instructor and piloted C-141s, graduating from the Air Force Test Pilot School at Edwards Air Force Base in 1990, where she was the class leader. She flew in Operation Urgent Fury in Grenada and has well over 4,000 hours in thirty different types of aircraft. Despite the groundbreaking position she earned in 1995, there was more to be done—even though she was the shuttle pilot that day, the position of flight commander was still occupied by a male.

As another class of astronauts was chosen, Wendy Lawrence, a 1981 graduate of the U.S. Naval Academy, was asked to join the corps. Her hero was her father, retired Navy Vice Admiral William P. Lawrence. He was reportedly one of the thirty-two Mercury candidates in the original 1959 test group at the Lovelace Clinic in Albuquerque, New Mexico. Commander Wendy Lawrence earned a master's degree from MIT in ocean engineering, and she was one of the first women helicopter pilots to go on deployment with a carrier battle group in the Indian Ocean.

Lawrence has flown three space shuttle missions. Her second mission was scheduled to drop her for an extended stay on the Russian space station *Mir*. The *Mir* had fallen casualty to several disasters prior to her blastoff and repairs necessitated by these catastrophes required that all hands be available to suit up in a Russian space suit in support of repairs or in an emergency. Since the Russian space suit, unlike those built for the Americans, was not proportioned for short women, there was considerable concern that Lawrence couldn't safely fit into it. A former Soviet astronaut who was familiar with the Russian space suit called Lawrence "a small fragile sparrow," declaring it unsafe for her to go. After several agonizing days of consultation, NASA, who had feared considerable public female backlash, replaced her with a man whose physical stature was more compatible with the space suit. This decision, made only two months prior to the launch and after a year of training, was an unexpected disappointment for Lawrence, but she supported it completely by maintaining that the change had nothing to do with her gender, but only her size.

Catherine Coleman received a Ph.D. from the University of Massachusetts and is a captain in the Air Force. Before becoming an astronaut in 1992, Catherine (or "Cady" as she is known to friends) forged new paths for women in the physiological endurance arena. Like her Mercury Thirteen predecessors who set endurance records in the sensory deprivation tests thirty years before, Cady set several endurance and tolerance records as she participated in the physiological and new equipment studies of the centrifuge at the Armstrong Aeromedical Laboratory at Wright-Patterson Air Force Base.

The class of 1996 distinguished itself in many ways, one of which was the fact that there were eight women in its ranks. They held degrees ranging from zoology to aerospace engineering. U.S. space exploration continues to excel; in 1997, the spacecraft *Pathfinder* made its way to Mars on a quest to open up new venues of space exploration and hopefully provide new dreams for classes of women astronauts of the future. One of the latest groups of astronauts that might reap the benefits of the spaceship *Pathfinder* is the class of 1998, which consists of twenty-five personnel, four of whom are women. Barbara Morgan, who holds a bachelor's degree in biology from Stanford, is the next teacher-in-space candidate, succeeding Christa McAuliffe. She will train as an astronaut and will conduct school lessons while in space for children on earth.

Some of the forty-three women astronauts married other astronauts, and the possibility of couples in space became even more real; some of the speculation of the original portrayals in the 1960s press were borne out. There have been six couples at various times in which both partners were astronauts fully qualified to go into space on a shuttle mission. Sally Ride married Steven Hawley and Margaret Seddon married Robert Gibson. Anna and William Fisher were married before they entered the space program, while Steven Nagel and Linda Godwin married after they had entered the corps. Mark Lee and Jan Davis and Bonnie Dunbar and Ronald Sega also married after they became astronauts. To date, Mark Lee and Jan Davis have been the only husband-and-wife team to fly together on a shuttle mission. As one might imagine, their flight initiated lots of speculation in the mass-media connected with "matrimonial relations in space." They had no comment.

Despite every effort Mercury Thirteen members Jan and Marion Dietrich made to become the first set of twins in the space program, they were never seriously considered. Twins in the astronaut corps became a reality when the class of 1996 was chosen and identical twins Mark and Scott Kelly were named as astronauts. The press establishment again began to wildly speculate at the possibilities. It is sad to contemplate the advantages that aviation medicine could have reaped from the study of two identical organisms that had traveled into space. If NASA had taken advantage of the opportunity provided them thirty-five years earlier in 1961 with the Dietrich twins, a quantum leap in understanding the physiology of space travel could have been achieved. In addition to these creative possibilities, there is now speculation in the press as to when the first all-female shuttle crew will be making history.

The class of 1995 was notable in that two of the five women chosen to become astronauts were selected to serve alongside Eileen Collins as pilots. Pamela Melroy came to NASA by way of Desert Storm and the Air Force Test Pilot School at Edwards Air Force Base. Her educational credentials are equally as outstanding as her flying credentials. From the time she was eleven years old, she could only think of flying. She earned an undergraduate degree from Wellesley College and a master's degree in earth and planetary sciences from MIT while logging over 4,000 hours in forty-five different aircraft.

United States Navy Lieutenant Commander Susan Still-Kilrain was also chosen as a shuttle pilot. She earned a graduate degree in aerospace engineering from the Georgia Institute of Technology while working full-time for Lockheed Martin Corporation. From there, she was commissioned into the Navy and became an aviator. She is a distinguished graduate of the U.S. Naval Test Pilot School and has been trained to fly the F-14 Tomcat Navy jet. Originally assigned to a fighter squadron at Naval Air Station Oceana in Virginia Beach, Virginia, after joining NASA, she has piloted the shuttle twice, once in April 1997 and again in July 1997 taking her and her crew 6.2 million miles around the earth.

Eileen Collins just previous to her history-making flight as the commander of Space
Shuttle Mission STS-93—a five-day mission, launched in July, 1999, aboard Space
Shuttle Columbia. (courtesy NASA)

Chapter Sixteen

In what may be one of the last notable milestones for women in space, on July 23, 1999, onboard the shuttle *Columbia*, once again Eileen Collins flew into space, this time as the first woman commander of an American spacecraft. She led an international, multicultural crew on a mission to launch the most advanced X-ray telescope of its kind ever to be flown. When the mission was announced, flight commander Collins went out of her way to pay homage, for the second time, to all the women who had come before her, including "the Mercury women from back in the early 1960s that went through all the tough medical testing to become the first astronauts." Once again she very graciously invited the thirteen women to view the launch at the Cape in Florida. While there, Janie Hart remembers an encounter with Eileen's father. He confessed to being apprehensive before the launch; not about his daughter's capabilities of piloting the shuttle, but for her safety. After three failed launch attempts, Collins took the shuttle up into the sky, with the women's hearts along for the ride. The NASA announcer heralded the trip with the words, "And we have liftoff, reaching new heights for women and astronomy." Even American men were affected. One of the original members of the Lovelace Clinic testing team confessed to having swelled up "like a bullfrog" when he saw the launch that day.

Collins's ability to keep her cool was tested time and again as several problems popped up at inopportune moments during the launch.

An electrical short disabled a set of the engine computers, one of the instrument displays went dark, and the shuttle ran out of gas before it reached the planned altitude, but Collins never displayed anything but competence.

In an unexpected salute from an old enemy, a few days into the mission, Collins was hailed by Commander Viktor Afanasyev, who was aboard the *Mir* space station: "I would like to congratulate you from the bottom of my heart. You are a courageous woman." Subsequent to her return, Collins was asked about what her young daughter thought of her job. Collins said that apparently she thinks everyone's mother is a shuttle pilot.

An underlying theme throughout the two eras of women's endeavors in the world of space travel is the constant understanding that all the women carried inside themselves the belief that they were unique and had to serve as a model to all who watched and waited to see if they could actually carry their portion of the burden. The Mercury Thirteen were told they were not competent to do so, but the next generation of women were at least given the chance. They are succeeding magnificently while citing numerous reasons for their admission into the astronaut corps. Some believe that timing and luck had an enormous bearing on who was chosen into the various classes. Others credit the women's movement that swept the country during the 1960s and 1970s. Still others thank the Mercury Thirteen for planting the seed in the consciousness of the nation as well as NASA.

At a celebration of the twenty-fifth anniversary of the thirteen women's foray into astronaut testing, Sally Ride wrote them a letter praising their bravery and willingness to try to break the barriers that held them earthbound, as well as those which might have stood in the way of women like Ride if they had not gone before. Her letter reads, in part: "I'm sorry my schedule does not permit me to be present at today's ceremony honoring all of you who participated in the Lovelace astronaut testing program some twenty-five years ago. I wish

I could be there to personally congratulate and applaud you for your diligence, foresight, and dedication to having women recognized as potential contributors to this nation's space program. I know you volunteered your time and efforts at considerable professional and personal inconvenience. I would like to assure you that, although you were not able to realize your collective goal, your accomplishments demonstrated that women could perform and achieve in space and helped open the door for those of us who followed." These words are treasured even today; this acknowledgment, by one of the best, was an imprimatur of excellence on the Mercury Thirteen.

The men of the old NASA have also softened a bit as these incredibly credentialed women have come into the space program. Former astronaut Alan Bean noted that the women have fit in faster than expected. In 1980 he said, "Two years ago I thought they'd be women in space suits trying to act like men in space suits. Well, I was wrong. It's just as natural for a woman to be in a space suit as it is for a man." Would that anyone had said that forty years ago for the Mercury Thirteen women! Bean and many others developed a newfound appreciation and understanding that women are just as capable as men in the astronaut field, but not all the earlier astronauts have followed suit. For some, old habits die hard. In Washington, D.C. during a March 1999 presentation of his newly published book, *Last Man on the Moon,* former astronaut Eugene Cernan repeatedly urged the young male military officers in the audience to consider becoming astronauts and pursuing Mars exploration. He did this, inconsiderately, numerous times despite the myriad of female ranking officers who were also present.

A total of forty-three women are presently serving or who have served in the NASA astronaut corps or have done so in the past. Three of these have been chosen to participate as pilots. NASA is proud of its post–1978 record for recruiting and training women astronauts. Congratulating themselves might be premature. Consider that from

May 5, 1961, until February 20, 1962 (a mere ten months), three men were allowed to command this country's spaceships. Now consider that from May 5, 1961, until the present, a span of over forty years, only one woman has been allowed to command an American spaceship. Only a total of three women have been chosen as pilots compared to dozens of men. Taking into account the number of talented women pilots this country has to offer from the military academies, military flight training programs, private programs, and test pilot schools, it seems that NASA is still far behind in its gender-neutral strategy. When the announcement was made by First Lady Hillary Rodham Clinton that Collins was to be the commander of STS-93, the American Astronautical Society's editorial in the *Space Times* congratulated her. The editorial also congratulated NASA on the choice, saying, "It's an important step toward overcoming the gender bias that has historically been so much a part of engineering and science." Despite efforts, there is arguably a gender bias that seems to be alive and well in the astronaut pilots' and commanders' ranks that still must be addressed by NASA.

Another exciting aspect of the space industry that may provide a way for many women to experience space travel is just beginning to become feasible. Because so many strides have been made in the technology of spacecraft, a tiny but intense group of people has begun viewing space as the next tourist destination and commercial workplace. The January 1, 2000, *Aviation Week & Space Technology* magazine quotes former Lockheed Martin chairman Norman Augustine on the importance of space as a tourist destination: 'The most important space development will be the advent of a burgeoning tourist industry to near-Earth orbit." In many cases, this budding segment of the tourism business sees space as replacing the conventional sea-cruise vacation. There are three commercial U.S. land-based spaceports—one in Florida, one in California, and one in Virginia—and there is one sea-based launch facility. The dream is to use these

(top left) Wally Funk in mid-1990s: (right) Wally Funk (right side, upside down) in Russia, experiencing weightlessness, 2000: (lower left) Wally Funk staying in shape swimming with the dolphins as Sea World in 2001. (courtesy Wally Funk)

four and other international facilities to launch tourists into space for the ultimate getaway; maybe one of the thirteen women will be on the first flight. As the Cold War blows warm, sharing of space opportunities with the Russian government is becoming relatively common. Seeking another experience to enhance the possibility of ultimately going into space, Wally Funk has wrangled training opportunities in various Russian facilities. She spent a week in 2000 training at the Yuri Gagarin Cosmonaut Training facility in Star City, Russia, where she spent ten hours a day attending briefings on the full-sized equipment including the *Mir.* Wally has never let go of her original dream and is still expecting to go into space one day. She is greatly respected for her efforts which were reflected in a report in the July 27, 2000 *Taos News* stating that the most touching part of her week in Russia was, "when cosmonaut Valery Korzun removed his uniformed space pin with ribbon and pinned it on her."

Chapter Seventeen

On October 29, 1998, NASA gave John Glenn a return ride into space. This "mission" was ostensibly to study the aging human body in outer space. It was not a mission that was demanded by the public or research organizations, but instead seems to have been the dream ride of an aging astronaut who has never lost the thrill of being America's hero. According to NASA officials, the need for this kind of research was "Glenn's idea" and the fact that he was a senator with weighty political connections made it an enormous plus for them to say yes. He is said to have badgered the director of NASA for two years until NASA finally relented. His presence on this shuttle mission was less than thrilling for a lot of people, including some of the 121 active astronauts in

NASA launch of Space Shuttle Mission STS-95 on October 29, 1998, with John Glenn aboard. (courtesy NASA)

NASA's stable. Reported at the time in the *Dayton Daily News*, they, " . . . resent the fact that Glenn is taking up what could have been their shuttle seat." Other critics termed the flight of *STS-95* and the use of large amounts of tax dollars as the "ultimate junket," saying that even some of his phalanx of supporters, " . . . believe the science research is just an excuse to give him one more glorious ride across the heavens."

In the face of this criticism, proponents point out that NASA has long sought to study conditions in space and relate them to those on earth so that life can be improved for all mankind. They have sought through experiments and studies to translate specific benefits for targeted populations into better medical applications on earth. In fact, NASA has worked closely with the likes of the National Institutes of Health (NIH) National Institute on Aging to begin to bring some of the value of space study home to benefit earth's aging population. Senator Glenn is old enough to participate in a study of aging, but a study of one person is not sufficient to gain adequate knowledge to make major changes in medical protocol used for an entire population. If the study is continued with additional subjects, and if benefit is gained for the earth's population in general, it will have been worth it. Testing one subject, though, will probably not provide enough data to ensure success.

Glenn's return to the astronaut ranks created another bit of irony for the Mercury Thirteen. Despite vigorous argument during the July 1962 Congressional hearings about the amount of training required to be an astronaut, Glenn chose to train for this mission only during breaks in his congressional schedule. A *Dayton Daily News* article written by Timothy Gaffney stated he ignored admonishments that the shuttle is "vastly more complex than the tiny *Mercury* capsule Glenn flew in 1962," and the training requirements should have been at least tenfold those for the *Mercury* capsule. His capsule had 8 buttons, 19 indicator lights, and 56 switches; the shuttle has 219 buttons, 559 indicator lights, and 2,325 switches. His 1962-era assertion of time-consuming training requirements seems now to have been an argument of convenience to keep women from gaining admission to the space program. Since he disregarded his own words, one wonders if he considered whether his tailored training schedule potentially put the lives of the crew in danger.

Legendary U.S. astronaut Storey Musgrave, who at the age of sixty was forced from the ranks of active astronauts after six space missions, was openly critical of Glenn's training schedule, saying, "Like anything else, you get out of it what you put in." Musgrave went on to point out that, unlike Glenn, even though he was retired at the age of sixty-one, "I cared about space enough to do it for thirty years. The important thing is, I cared enough about space to stay with it. People need to look at it like that. I did not leave for greener pastures, then come back as a passenger." Even though harsh, Musgrave's words were not the first instance Glenn had been criticized for his lack of time "in the saddle." After his groundbreaking flight in 1962, he began making so many public appearances that he was no longer putting the normal time into training. Astronaut Wally Schirra made note of this in a television interview, saying that Glenn was shirking his duties. Training, then and now, is generally required full-time for at least a year prior to a flight.

Musgrave stated that he actually supported Glenn's return to space, but just wished that everyone would give name to what it actually was. He called it "the right thing to do" because of the history involved. But, he added, "we need to be honest about it. We are flying a legislative passenger, as we have in the past. It's John Glenn. Marvelous. But it is a legislative passenger."

Time away from the space program seems to have provided Glenn with some clouded memories as well. During the intense press coverage prior to his return flight, Glenn was asked many times about his role in denying the Mercury Thirteen places in the astronaut corps. He complained that he had been made the "fall guy" for why the women were not allowed into NASA. Glenn said only weeks before his second flight, "They've made me the hit guy for why women were not in space." He insisted he had made only one remark at a congressional hearing in 1962 and that he had been considered the "bad guy" ever since. His testimony in its entirety as it was recorded in the *Congressional Record*, however, shows that he contributed more than just a single offhand remark about the appropriateness of the Mercury Thirteen being allowed into the ranks. He repeatedly made negative comments toward the women and never once indicated support in any way for them or their inclusion into the space program. He used an analogy about the women being physically fit, but not being astronaut material, saying, "My mother would have been able to come to Washington and pass the physical, but she probably couldn't play for the Redskins."

The fact that NASA agreed to allow John Glenn to go back into space even though he was well over seventy years old has spurred a movement to allow at least one of the original thirteen women to go also. They are in the same age range as Glenn and would be excellent specimens to study the physiologic differences between the aging of men and that of women. Medical science has long gotten away with carrying out testing and clinical trials on men only, with benefits for men only. Demand is rising, however, for age-related testing to be done on women as well as men. This demand includes equivalent testing in space. What better test group than the Mercury Thirteen women? With their medical baselines established during the Lovelace tests, they would make excellent test subjects, and every one of them, it seems, would be willing. Janie Hart, who is the same age as Glenn, said when asked if she would go into space that not only would she, but that she could pass the physical with a blood pressure of 130 over 80. Jerri Truhill is also as willing today as she was then, and wants all of the remaining women astronaut candidates to have the chance to train to see if they can win a seat on a future shuttle. Gene Nora

Jessen is also ready to go, pointing out, "I have every intention of living long enough to travel in space one day as a passenger." And of course, Wally Funk has never quit actively pursuing a seat into space on U.S., Russian, or commercial vessels.

When asked to comment on this new mission for Glenn, Funk was characteristically blunt. She pointed out that by abruptly adding John Glenn to the flight roster, NASA had probably cost another member of the original team his or her place on the flight: "I feel bad that he took a spot away from a young astronaut who had probably waited three or four years for that slot. He's already had his ticker-tape parade." She admitted, though, that with Glenn's political clout NASA had no option other than to say yes.

On hearing of Glenn's latest flight, Jerrie left her missionary work in the Amazon in the hopes that NASA might once again lend a sympathetic ear to her quest to go into space. She said from the beginning that she doesn't want a token ride; she simply wants the same deal John Glenn received—the right to go into space to participate in the study of the aging human body: "If they think that it's important to study an older man, I can't see why it's not important to study an older woman." When asked if she thought NASA "owed" her a space ride, she replied that NASA did not owe her anything.

That's not what some of her friends and supporters think. A campaign was launched to convince then-NASA director Dan Goldin that at least one of the original thirteen women should be tested to determine if she is capable of going into space, and when she completes the tests successfully, a seat on a future shuttle mission should be saved for her. The National Organization for Women (NOW) has begun a letter-writing and petition-signing campaign nationwide with the hopes of getting Jerrie a seat on a shuttle flight. NOW's president, Patricia Ireland, stated that the organization she heads chose to support Jerrie's efforts because NASA denied her a chance to go into space years earlier solely because she was a woman. That was then, but this is now, and the same excuse shouldn't be allowed to prevail a second time. Even though the campaign has centered on Jerrie Cobb, all the women would dearly love the chance to go.

Even former First Lady Hillary Rodham Clinton had an early interest in becoming an astronaut. She tells a story about herself when she was fourteen years old and was inspired by Alan Shepard's heroics. Clinton says she wrote to NASA inquiring about the requirements for a young lady to become an astronaut. They informed her, as they had many others, that NASA did not consider women. Her interest has continued and at her request, NASA Director Dan Goldin met with Jerrie to discuss her continued aspirations of becoming an astronaut. As she journeyed to the meeting, Jerrie said, her mind was reeling with the possibilities of what the outcome of the meeting might be; once again, however, fate was in a dark mood, and it turned into a simple social call with Goldin admitting that he had precipitated the meeting only as a courtesy to Clinton. A spokesperson from NASA put the matter into harsh perspective by saying, "It would be nice to be able to fly Jerrie Cobb as a consolation, but that's not going to happen. We've honored these women. Nobody wants to slight their accomplishments. But they were misled into believing they would become astronaut candidates. We weren't the ones who misled them, and we can't make up for it."

Hope was reborn in a statement provided in September 1998 at the occasion of the grand reopening of the Pioneer Women Museum in Ponca City, Oklahoma. During the presentation, U.S. Senator James Inhofe spoke of Jerrie's accomplishments and even of the hopes that NASA had for her future. While Jerrie sat speechless, Inhofe provided the crowd with a quote from Administrator Goldin: "If everything goes well and the data comes in after the John Glenn senior citizen space flight and the data works out, we will be doing it again. It is logical that a woman would be next and there is no one in America that is more qualified and deserving to be in that space shuttle than Jerrie Cobb."

Jerrie is philosophical about it and refuses to give up the dream that all thirteen women had forty years ago. She said, "You can't give up a dream that you feel is really your destiny." Her sister, Carolyn Warren Lawrence, agrees: "This means everything to her. This is her lifelong dream." And so once again after all these years, the question still waiting to be answered comes down to, "Is there space for women?"

Appendix

Table 1. Credentials of U.S. Women Astronauts

Mission Specialist	Bachelor's Degree	Master's Degree	Doctorate
Class of 1978			
Sally Ride	Physics— Stanford	Physics— Stanford	Physics— Stanford
Margaret Seddon	Physiology— Berkeley		Medical– University of Tennessee
Kathryn Sullivan	Earth sciences— University of California		Geology Dalhousie University
Shannon Lucid	Chemistry— University of Oklahoma	Biochemistry— University of Oklahoma	Biochemistry— University of Oklahoma
Judith Resnik	Electrical engineering— Carnegie-Mellon		Electrical engineering— University of Maryland
Anna Fisher	Chemistry— University of California at Los Angeles	Chemistry— University of California at Los Angeles	Medical— University of California at Los Angeles
Class of 1980			
Mary Cleave	Biological sciences— Colorado State	Microbia ecology— Utah State	Civil and environmental engineering— Utah State
Bonnie Dunbar	Ceramic engineering— University of Washington	Ceramic engineering— University of Washington	Biomedical engineering— University of Houston

Class of 1984

Ellen Baker	Geology—State University of New York, Buffalo	Public health—University of Texas	Medical—Cornell
Marsha Ivins	Aerospace engineering—University of Colorado		
Kathryn Thornton	Physics—Auburn University	Physics—University of Virginia	Physics—University of Virginia

Class of 1985

Tamara Jernigan	Physics—Stanford	Engineering science—Stanford Astronomy – University of California at Berkeley	Physics and astronomy—Rice University
Linda Godwin	Math and physics—Southeast Missouri State	Physics—University of Missouri	Physics—University of Missouri

Class of 1987

Jan Davis	Applied biology—Georgia Institute of Technology Mechanical engineering—Auburn	Mechanical engineering—University of Alabama	Mechanical engineering—University of Alabama
Mae Jemison	Chemical engineering—Stanford		Medical—Cornell

Class of 1990

Susan Helms	Aeronautical engineering—United States Air Force Academy	Aeronautics—Stanford	
Janice Voss	Electrical engineering—Purdue	Electrical engineering—Massachusetts Institute of Technology	Aeronautics—Massachusetts Institute of Technology
Nancy Sherlock	Biological science—Ohio State	Safety engineering—University of Southern California	Industrial engineering—University of Houston
Ellen Ochoa	Physics—San Diego State University	Electrical engineering—Stanford	Electrical engineering—Stanford

Class of 1992

Catherine Coleman	Chemistry—Massachusetts Institute of Technology		Polymer science and engineering—University of Massachusetts
Mary E. Weber	Chemical engineering—Purdue		Physical chemistry—University of California at Berkeley
Wendy Lawrence	Ocean engineering—United States Naval Academy	Ocean engineering—Massachusetts Institute of Technology	

Class of 1994

Kathryn Hire	Engineering and management— United States Naval Academy	Space technology— Florida Institute of Technology	
Kalpana Chawla	Aeronautical engineering— Punjab Engineering College	Aerospace engineering— University of Texas	Aerospace engineering— University of Colorado
Janet Kavandi	Chemistry— Missouri Southern State College		Chemistry— University of Washington

Class of 1996

Laurel Clark	Zoology— University of Wisconsin		Medical— University of Wisconsin
Yvonne Cagle	Biochemistry— San Francisco State University		Medical— University of Washington
Lisa Nowak	Aerospace engineering— United States Naval Academy	Aeronautical engineering and astronautical engineering— United States Naval Postgraduate School	
Sandra Magnus	Physics— University of Missouri	Electrical engineering— University of Missouri	Engineering— Georgia Institute of Technology

Joan Higginbotham	Electrical engineering— Southern Illinois University	Management and space systems— Florida Institute of Technology	
Stephanie Wilson	Engineering science— Harvard	Aerospace engineering— University of Texas	
Peggy Whitson	Biology/ chemistry— Iowa Wesleyan College		Biochemistry— Rice University
Heidemarie Stefanyshyn-Piper	Mechanical engineering— MIT	Mechanical engineering— MIT	
Class of 1998			
Tracy Caldwell	Chemistry— California State, Fullerton University		Chemistry— University of California at Davis
Patricia Hilliard	Biology— Indiana University of Pennsylvania		Medical— Medical College of Pennsylvania
Barbara Morgan (teacher)	Human biology— Stanford		
Sunita Williams	Physical sciences— United States Naval Academy	Engineering management— Florida Institute of Technology	

Class of 2000

K. Megan McArthur	Aerospace engineering—University of California at Los Angeles		Oceanography—University of California at San Diego
Karen L. Nyberg	Mechanical engineering—University of North Dakota	Mechanical engineering—University of Texas	Mechanical engineering—University of Texas
Nicole Passonno Stott	Aeronautical engineering—Embry-Riddle University	Engineering management—University of Central Florida	

Pilots

Class of 1990

Eileen Collins (pilot)	Math and economics—Syracuse University	Operations research—Stanford Space systems management—Webster University	

Class of 1994

Susan Still-Kilrain (pilot)	Aeronautical engineering—Embry-Riddle University	Aerospace engineering—Georgia Institute of Technology	
Pamela Melroy (pilot)	Physics and astronomy—Wellesley College	Earth and planetary sciences—Massachusetts Institute of Technology	

Chronology: Training of Women Astronauts

October 4, 1957—*Sputnik* launched.

April 1959—Mercury Seven names are announced.

September 1959—Jerrie Cobb was first approached to become a subject in the "Women in Space" testing program in Albuquerque.

February 15–20, 1960—Jerrie Cobb underwent phase I testing at the Lovelace Clinic in Albuquerque.

August 18, 1960—Dr. Lovelace attended a meeting in Stockholm and revealed Jerrie's test results to the public.

September 1960—Jerrie Cobb went into phase II testing at the Veterans Administration Hospital in Oklahoma City.

February 1961—Jan and Marion Dietrich go through phase I testing.

Spring 1961—Other women chosen for testing go to Albuquerque.

May 5, 1961—Alan Shepard was the first American in space.

May 15–23, 1961—Jerrie went through phase III testing at Navy facilities at Pensacola, Florida.

June–July 1961—Mary Wallace Funk and Rhea Allison underwent phase II testing at the Veterans Administration Hospital in Oklahoma City.

Summer 1961—All thirteen women applicants signed the waivers for phase III testing.

September 15, 1961—The Navy notified Dr. Lovelace of cancellation of tests.

September 17, 1961—Meeting with all thirteen applicants had been scheduled in Pensacola for this Sunday afternoon. Some were already en route before being notified that the meeting and all of the tests had been cancelled.

September 18, 1961—Date on which phase III tests had been scheduled for the thirteen women.

September 1961—NASA provided numerous explanations as to why the testing had been cancelled.

February 20, 1962—John Glenn orbited the earth.

May 24, 1962—Scott Carpenter orbited the earth.

July 17–19, 1962—Jerrie Cobb and Janie Hart testified at Congressional subcommittee hearings; actually held for only two days.

June 16, 1963—Valentina Tereshkova was the first woman in space aboard *Vostok 6.*

June 1978—The first women (including Sally Ride) were chosen to serve in the U.S. space program.

April 12, 1981—First manned mission on shuttle *STS-1* (*Columbia*) launched.

June 18, 1983—Sally Ride becomes the first U.S. woman in space aboard *STS-7* (*Challenger*).

January 28, 1986—Space shuttle *Challenger* exploded seconds after launch, killing all aboard including Judith A. Resnik (mission specialist) and Christa McAuliffe (payload specialist).

February 3, 1995—Eileen Collins became the first woman to pilot an American spacecraft on the shuttle flight *STS-63.*

March 22, 1996—Space shuttle *Atlantis* docked and dropped Shannon Lucid at the Russian space station *Mir.* Lucid was the first female astronaut to crew a space station.

September 26, 1996—Space shuttle *Atlantis* picked up Shannon Lucid and touched down on this date, making her the U.S. astronaut and the woman who had been in space longer than anyone else.

January 16, 1998—NASA announced that seventy-seven-year-old former astronaut John Glenn was returning to the astronaut corps for one more trip into space. As a payload specialist, he would study the effects of space on the aging human body.

October 29, 1998—John Glenn returned to space more than thirty-six years after he became the first American man to orbit the earth.

July 23, 1999—Eileen Collins became the first woman to command a U.S. spacecraft on the shuttle flight *STS-93*.

Bibliography

Books

Atkinson, Joseph D., Jr. and Jay M. Shafritz. *The Real Stuff: A History of NASA's Astronaut Recruitment Program.* New York: Praeger Scientific, 1985.

Briggs, Carole S. *Women in Space, Reaching the Last Frontier.* Minneapolis: Lerner Publications, 1983.

Brinley, Maryann Bucknum and Jacqueline Cochran. *Jackie Cochran.* New York: Bantam Books, 1987.

Chaikan, Andrew. *A Man on the Moon.* New York: Viking Press, 1994.

Cobb, Jerrie and Jane Rieker. *Woman into Space.* Englewood Cliffs, New Jersey: Prentice-Hall, Inc., 1963.

Compton, William David. *Where No Man Has Gone Before.* Washington, D.C.: NASA Office of Management, Scientific and Technical Information Division, 1989.

Fox, Mary Virginia. *Women Astronauts Aboard the Shuttle.* New York: Julian Messner Publications, 1984.

Haynsworth, Leslie and David Toomey. *Amelia Earhart's Daughters.* New York: William Morrow and Company, Inc., 1998.

Holden, Henry M. and Captain Lori Griffith. *Ladybirds II.* Mt. Freedom, N.J.: Black Hawk Publishing Co., 1993.

McGuire, Nina and Sandra Wallus Sammons. *Jacqueline Cochran; America's Fearless Aviator.* Lake Buena Vista, Fla.: Tailored Tours Publications, 1997.

National Aeronautics and Space Administration. *NASA Photography Index.* Washington, D.C.: NASA Public Affairs Division, 1987.

O'Connor, Karen. *Sally Ride and the New Astronauts: Scientists in Space.* New York: Franklin Watts, 1983.

Paszkiewicz, Dennis. *The Nazi Rocketeers.* Westport, Conn.: Praeger Publishing, 1995.

Phillips, Cabell. *Decade of Triumph and Trouble: The 1940s.* New York: Macmillan Publishing Company, 1975.

Swenson, Lloyd S., Jr., James M. Grimwood, and Charles C. Alexander. *This New Ocean.* Washington, D.C.: NASA Public Affairs Division, 1998.

Weiser, William J. *The Space Guidebook.* New York: Coward-McCann, Inc., 1960.

Wolfe, Tom. *The Right Stuff.* New York: Farrar, Straus, Giroux, 1979.

Wright, Mike. *What They Didn't Teach You about World War II.* Novato, Calif: Presidio Press, 1998.

Congressional Documents

Gruening, Ernest. "Girl Cosmonaut a Soviet Triumph." *Congressional Record,* 27 June 1963.

House of Representatives, Special Subcommittee on the Selection of Astronauts, Committee on Science and Astronautics. *Qualifications for Astronauts,* 17 July 1962.

Karth, Joseph E., "Karth Scores NASA on Stalled Space Benefits Flights." Press release, 12 March 1969.

United States Senate Staff Report of the Committee on Aeronautical and Space Sciences. *Manned Space Flight Program of the National Aeronautics and Space Administration: Projects Mercury, Gemini, and Apollo.* 4 September 1962.

Periodicals

Author unknown. "From Aviatrix to Astronautrix." *Time,* 29 August 1960.

——"Female Astronauts." *Spaceflight,* April 1997.

——"Beyond the Earth." *Time,* 22 August, 1960.

——"The U.S. Team Is Still Warming Up the Bench." *Life,* 28 June 1963.

——"Beyond the Earth." *Time,* 22August 1960.

Black, James T. "Walking in Space." *Southern Living,* June 1997.

Collins, Mike. "Carrying the Fire." *Time,* 23September 1974.

Cooper, Gordon. "First Rocket We Will Ride." *Life,* 3 October 1960.

Cox, Donald. "Women Astronauts." *Space World,* September 1961.

Dietrich, Marion. "First Woman into Space." *McCall's,* September 1961.

Haskins, Mardell. "Irene Leverton—Mercury 13 Astronaut Candidate." *Aviation Report,* May 1998.

Kozloski, Lillian and Maura J. Mackowski. "The Wrong Stuff." *Final Frontier,* May/June 1995.

Luce, Clare Boothe. "But Some People Simply Never Get the Message." *Life,* 28 June 1963.

Mace, Dr. David R. "Does a Wife Have a Right to Work?" *McCall's,* October 1961.

McCullough, Joan. "13 Who Were Left Behind." *MS,* September 1973.

Pesavento, Peter. "From Aelita to the International Space Station." *Quest,* 8, no. 2, 2000.

Newspapers

Anderson, Jack. "Would-be Astronauts: Legion of Angry Women."

Associated Press. "Women in Space-Quotes," 1 February 1995.

Author unknown. "Women's Place in Outer Space," *The Washington Post,* 17 March 1968.

——"The Craftier Sex Is Cleared for Space." *Los Angeles Times,* 26 August 1960.

——"Girl 'in Space' Six Days Without a Hallucination." *Chicago Daily Tribune,* 6 November 1959.

——"Glenn—Musgrave." *Associated Press,* 3 October 1998.

Author unknown. "Is Woman's Place on Moon, Maybe?" *The Boston Globe,* 27 April 1965.

—— "New Astronaut Standards Urged." *The Baltimore Sun,* 15 February 1965:7.

—— "Women Astronauts Needed." *Newport News Times Herald,* 17 June 1963.

—— "13 Women Triumphing Vicariously." *New York Times,* 5 February 1995.

—— "Woman Space Pioneer." *Philadelphia Inquirer,* 15 January 1959.

—— "Russians Eager for U.S. Astronaut — 'to clean'." *USA Today,* 22 March 1996.

—— "Collins First Female Shuttle Commander." *The NASA Roundup*, 13 March 1998:1.

—— "Astronauts Are Just 'Fine'." *Washington Daily News*, 7 July 1959.

—— "Women's Place in Outer Space." *The Washington Post*, 17 March 1968.

—— "Congratulations to Eileen Collins: The First Woman to Command a Shuttle Mission." *Space Times*, June 1998.

Beyerlein, Tom. "1st Women Astronauts Aground." *Dayton Daily News*, 25 October 1991.

Boffey, Phillip M. "Despite Numbers of Applicants, Few Civilians Are Selected as Astronauts." *New York Times*, 7 August 1987.

Campbell, Heather. "Female Mercury Candidates Fly in for Centerville Reunion." *Centerville Bellbrook Times*, 30 October 1991.

Cross, James M. "Return of 'The Mercury 13.'" *The 99news/International Women Pilots*, March/April 1995.

Dunn, Marcia. "Out Front — Women in Space." *Associated Press*, 1 February 1995.

—— "NASA Pioneer Asks for Her Shot at Space." *Washington Post*, 13 July 1998.

Harwood, John. "Female Astros? Sure, Says Swigert." *New Haven Register*, 9 September 1970.

Haskins, Mardell. "Irene Leverton, Mercury 13 Astronaut Candidate." *Aviation Report*, May 1998.

Hines, William "Spacemen's Abilities Withering in Red Tape." *Washington Star*, 8 July 1959.

Lane, Earl. "Skylab Promises Humanized Astronauts." *Los Angeles Times*, 12 November 1978.

Macomber, Frank. "Can Space Lady Be Far Behind." *San Jose Mercury,* 26 July 1972.

Maloney, Jim. "Shuttle Precedents Secondary." *Washington Post,* 30 April 1982.

Merzer, Martin. "These Astronaut Trainees Never Left Earth." *Miami Herald,* 27 October 1998.

O'Toole, Thomas. "Thirty-Five New Guys." *Washington Post Magazine,* 20 July 1980.

Precker, Michael. "Shooting for the Stars." *Dallas Morning News,* 20 September 1998.

Rickman, Sarah. "IWASM Hosts 30th Reunion for Participants in First Women Astronaut Testing Program." *The International Women's Air and Space Museum Quarterly,* No. 4, 1991.

Ruark, Robert. "Let the Girls, Bless 'Em, Cut Loose in Space!"

Schefter, James. "Space Chores Awaiting the Touch of Women." *Washington Star,*

26 March 1981.

Spencer, Anne. "16 Astronauts Train at HAFB." *South Dade News Leader,* 1 August 1978.

Witkin, Richard. "Training for Space." *The New York Times,* 18 June 1963.

Interviews

Hart, Jane Phone interview with author from Mackinac Island, Michigan, 23 July 1998.

——Interview with author at her summer location in Mackinac Island, Michigan, 20 September 1999.

Kilgore, Dr. Donald. Phone interview with author from Albuquerque, New Mexico, 8 October 1999.

Truhill, Jerri. Phone interview with author from Ft. Worth, Texas, 27 July 1998.

Correspondence

Funk, Wally. 5 June 1998.

—— 5 August 1998.

Leverton, Irene. 20 August 1998.

Jessen, Gene Nora Stumbough. 29 July 1998.

Ratley,Sara Gorelick. 28 July 1998.

Cobb, Jerrie May. 1999.

Other

Clinkscales, A. Letter to NASA regional coordinators, 23 November 1976.

—— Letter to NASA director of personnel, 10 December 1976.

Cochran, Jacqueline. Letter to Jerrie Cobb, 23 March 1962.

Collins, Colonel Eileen. Transcript of comments made during White House ceremony,

6 March 1998.

Jessen, Gene Nora Stumbough. Documentation for the Dateline program on NBC, 1995.

Link, M. Mill and Donald K. Slayton. "Astronaut Selection and Training for Manned Space Flight" (draft), 1970.

National Aeronautics and Space Administration. *Invitation to Apply for Position of Research Astronaut-Candidate.* Announcement No. 1, 22 December 1958.

—— *Medical Selection for Astronauts and Space Crews,* undated.

—— *Operational Medical Support Program Checklist Flight Crew Medical Operations: Astronaut Selection,* undated.

—— Letter from Richard S. Johnston to Dr. G. M. Knauf. Subject: Space suit Capability Estimates, undated.

—— Letter from G. Dale Smith to Mr. George Low. Subject: Women Astronauts, 19 June 1961.

—— Letter from Hugh L. Dryden to Vice Admiral R. B. Pirie, 2 October 1961.

—— "Administrator's Memorandum on Equal Employment Opportunity," 20 February 1962.

—— "Women in NASA." Letter from George M. Low, 14 August 1973.

—— *The Early Years: Mercury to Apollo-Soyuz.* Information Summaries, PMS 001-A (KSC), May 1987.

—— "NASA Strategic Plan." 3 February 1996.

—— "Astronaut Selection and Training." Doc. No. NP199707006JSC, July 1997.

Personal letter from Irma Reynolds (citizen) to James Webb, 21 February 1965.

Ride, Dr. Sally K. Letter to the dedicated participants in the Lovelace Astronaut Testing Program, 24 October 1986.

Internet

Author unknown. "Glenn Sparks a Trend." *Dayton Daily News,* story archived on Internet without date.

Dietrick, Sandy. "Ovaries Not Included." Internet at www.hbo.com/apollo, 8 June 1998.

Gaffney, Timothy R. "Friendship 7 Pilot Sells NASA on a Return Trip to Space." *Dayton Daily News,* story archived on Internet without date.

— "Glenn Back in Training." *Dayton Daily News,* story archived on Internet without date.

Palmer, James. "Veteran Pilot Cagle Had Right Stuff Ahead of Her Time." *Macon Telegraph,* 1998. (Internet)

Index